CALLED TO CONTEND

AMERICA'S CONFLICT WITH GOD AND WHAT TO DO

DAVE WARN

Called to Contend is a wake-up call to the Church of America to understand the perilous situation in which we find ourselves. I so appreciate that this book does not leave us with an almost hopeless sense of the enormity of the evil we face. Dave Warn shares with us examples of what men, women, and young people are doing to drive back the evil in their local communities. Boldly, he also deals with the question that few attempt: What if God doesn't answer our prayers and heal our land? What then?! *Called to Contend* is a straightforward honest presentation of the why and how to contend for the faith, that neither dodges the hard questions nor minimizes the cost. I heartily endorse this book.

Dale Schlafer
Founder, The Center for World Revival and Awakening
Chairman of the Board emeritus, Promise Keepers

Copyright © 2024 DAVE WARN

Two Penny Publishing
850 E. Lime Street #266
Tarpon Springs, Florida 34688
TwoPennyPublishing.com
Info@TwoPennyPublishing.com

All rights reserved. No part of this publication may be reproduced, distributed, or transmitted in any form or by any means, including photocopying, recording, or other electronic or mechanical methods, without the prior written permission of the publisher, except by a reviewer who wishes to quote brief passages in connection with a review written for inclusion in a magazine, newspaper, website, or broadcast.

This book represents the personal views and opinions of the author and does not necessarily reflect the positions or opinions of the publisher. The content presented herein is based on the author's perspective and interpretation of the subject matter.

Unless otherwise indicated, all Scripture quotations are taken from the Holy Bible, New Living Translation (NLT®), Copyright © 1996, 2004, 2015 by Tyndale House Foundation. Used by permission of Tyndale House Publishers, Inc., Carol Stream, Illinois 60188.

Scripture quotations marked (ESV) are taken from The ESV® Bible (The Holy Bible, English Standard Version®), © 2001 by Crossway, a publishing ministry of Good News Publishers. Used by permission. All rights reserved."

Scripture quotations marked (NASB) are taken from the (NASB®) New American Standard Bible®, Copyright © 1960, 1971, 1977, 1995, 2020 by The Lockman Foundation. Used by permission. All rights reserved. lockman.org"

Scripture quotations marked (NIV) are taken from the Holy Bible, New International Version®, NIV®. Copyright © 1973, 1978, 1984, 2011 by Biblica, Inc.™ Used by permission of Zondervan. All rights reserved worldwide. www.zondervan.com The "NIV" and "New International Version" are trademarks registered in the United States Patent and Trademark Office by Biblica, Inc.™

Book Cover by Benjamin Rogers.

ISBN: 979-8-9901524-9-6
eBook also available

For permission requests and ordering information, email: info@twopennypublishing.com

For information about this author, to book event appearance, or media interview, please contact the author representative at: info@twopennypublishing.com

FIRST EDITION

Two Penny Publishing is a partnership publisher of a variety of genres. We help first-time and seasoned authors share their stories, passion, knowledge, and experiences that help others grow and learn. Please visit our website: TwoPennyPublishing.com if you would like us to consider your manuscript or book idea for publishing.

To those who follow Him who is Faithful and True.

Revelation 19:11

CONTENTS

Foreword viii
Introduction: A "Now" Message xi
1. The Need of the Hour. 1

Part One: What's Going On? 15

2. The Battle of the Ages. 17
3. Nations Matter 35
4. Our Greatest Threat 51
5. America in the Balance. 61
6. Have We Crossed a Line?. 75

Part Two: Fit for Service 97

7. Seeking 99
8. Standing 117
9. Suffering 129

Part Three: Called to Contend 149

10. Fighting the Good Fight 151
11. In the Church 161
12. In Society 179
13. In Government 203
14. Time to Overcome 225

About the Author 235
Notes. 237
Other Books by Dave Warn 251

FOREWORD

I first met Dave Warn in 2008 when he was directing The Institute of Campus Revival and Awakening at Yale University. We didn't keep in close touch after the institute, but when I heard years later that Dave had started his own ministry, *Forerunners of America*, I was amazed.

As someone in ministry, I know how hard it is to deliver just one message of judgment and warning. Sadly, many Christian ministers don't have the faith and strength to do it at all. But to build an entire ministry on this calling takes supernatural faith that I've rarely seen in Western Christianity. How can such a ministry even survive in this day of feel-good messages? Dave had the boldness to answer God's call and launch *Forerunners of America*, which makes me think that he is walking in the footsteps of biblical men of God like Jeremiah and Noah.

There were many other prophets, teachers, and preachers in Jeremiah's day. The vast majority told the people not to worry about the threat of the Babylonians. They assured the people that God would not punish them. No, God would only protect His people. After all, they were His chosen ones, rescued from Egypt, redeemed by His mighty right hand, and had the very Temple in their midst. "Peace, peace," was their message (Jeremiah 6:14; 8:11). But Jeremiah had a different message. It was not a popular one, but it was the necessary one and, most importantly, the one from God.

In colonial America, brave preachers gave messages that became known as "jeremiads," alerting people to God's impending judgment if they did not repent. Perhaps the most famous jeremiad was Jonathan Edwards' "Sinners in the Hands of an Angry God." This sermon stirred people to return to God and helped foment America's First Great Awakening. Thousands of souls were saved, and the future of a new nation would be incredibly blessed by this one sermon. But what if Jonathan Edwards and others like him didn't have the courage to be like Jeremiah?

I couldn't help but think of Dave Warn when I recently read Charles Spurgeon's sermon on Noah's faith from Hebrews: "By faith Noah, being warned by God concerning events as yet unseen, in reverent fear constructed an ark for the saving of his household. By this he condemned the world and became an heir of the righteousness that comes by faith" (Hebrews 11:7 ESV).

Spurgeon noted that Noah's faith was especially remarkable because he believed a word of warning. Many are willing to believe a message of comfort, but few are willing to receive a word of warning, and then to build their entire lives and ministry around that word.

If you don't know Dave, I want to make a few personal observations. Dave is not the kind of person you might expect. He doesn't seek out confrontation. He's not argumentative. He's not bitter, unpleasant, or filled with negativity. He is a kind and enjoyable person. In my mind, his ministry and message pour forth compassion as much as they pour forth God's severity (Romans 11:22).

He is also a man who earnestly seeks after God. Dave regularly participates and gives leadership in the Heritage Pastors Association's monthly days of prayer. We spend an entire day once a month seeking

God in prayer, fasting, repentance, and Scripture reading. Dave is a man of faith, conviction, and courage. This is why I'm always pleased to commend his ministry and his faith, similar to how God did with Noah. But may we all be unlike Noah's generation, which rejected God's message and paid dearly for it.

Dave was a forerunner to me and my colleagues at the Institute of Campus Revival and Awakening. He saw things that we had not yet seen. Thankfully, once we did, it made an enormous difference in our lives and ministries. Also, Dave has been a forerunner to many in what you are about to read. Pray that God will prepare your heart to receive this message and respond in greater faith!

Chuck Hetzler, Ph.D.
Discipleship Pastor
The Crossing
Quincy, Illinois

A "NOW" MESSAGE

It is difficult to read the Bible without becoming uneasy about America's future. All but a few of its sixty-six books imply or clearly state that people or nations that behave the way America is behaving right now are in trouble. This trouble is different from a poor choice that any one of us might make in our daily lives. This trouble is rooted in the reality that America is in conflict with God.

Because of this reality, we desperately need a "now" message from heaven—a message I have done my best to express in the following pages. Receiving insight that was important to previous generations is helpful, but it will not suffice as the fresh manna you and I need today. When looking deep inside, I believe receiving God's message for this day and hour—God's "now" message—is what many of us are longing for.

By delivering a "now" message, I am not claiming to be on par with a biblical prophet. I would rather quote one than try to be one. Nevertheless, I believe God has a lot to say about America, specifically to the body of Christ within America. It is this message that I have tried to capture.

Part One covers the characteristics and implications of the day and hour we find ourselves. *Part Two* addresses who we need to be to contend for the faith in a hostile culture. *Part Three* is a call to action. Put together, this is a tall order for a relatively short book, so I need to frame what follows by invoking two passages.

First, Jesus reprimanded the people for not discerning the times: "When you see clouds beginning to form in the west, you say, 'Here comes a shower.' And you are right. When the south wind blows, you say, 'Today will be a scorcher.' And it is. You fools! You know how to interpret the weather signs of the earth and sky, but you don't know how to interpret the present times" (Luke 12:54–56).

Jesus' point is that there is such a thing as a "now" message, and—as it was during Jesus' earthly ministry—it is crying out all around us. Indeed, we will have to choose to ignore it to miss it. Many people do. Further, Jesus said this rebuke to "the crowds" (Luke 12:54 ESV)—not to a select group of church leaders, scholars, nor the "super-spiritual." Therefore, everyone must take discerning the hour seriously.

When God gives a "now" message, it often includes difficulty ahead. Because of the disturbing nature of such messages, our reaction is often to deflect them. We do not want our daily routine disrupted, and we want to get on with our lives. The psychological term for this response is normalcy bias. In the end, we continue in our deceived state and change nothing. Yet, Jesus expected His listeners to discern God's "now" message. The implications of those who did—and didn't—were enormous.

Second, we must remember the men of Issachar who "understood the times" and "knew what Israel should do" (1 Chronicles 12:32 NIV). Rather than denying the evil proliferating throughout culture or neglecting to carry out God's purposes, like these men, we must understand what is taking place and put feet to our beliefs.

To understand, yet do nothing, is not an option. Jesus *taught* the crowds, and He also *did things*. Jesus not only knew how to contend for the faith. *He did contend.*

James commanded Christians not to simply hear God's Word but to "do what it says" (James 1:22). Practical application of God's truth is necessary for every generation, but as we are about to see, these exhortations contain an almost unique urgency for us today.

Let me stop here so you can turn the page to what I believe is an important aspect of God's "now" message. While I am writing to Americans, if you are from another country, you will find many of the principles applicable to your nation. As the axiom teaches, "Methods are many, principles are few; methods often change, principles rarely do." May we all stick to biblical principles and seek God for precisely what to do.

THE NEED OF THE HOUR

> *Before he [Jesus] came, John the Baptist preached that all the people of Israel needed to repent of their sins and turn to God and be baptized. As John was finishing his ministry he asked, "Do you think I am the Messiah? No, I am not! But he is coming soon."*
>
> Acts 13:24–25

My colleague's tone was surprisingly serious. Wesley, a trusted friend, wanted to schedule an appointment with me. This formality was odd since we often chatted throughout the workday. *What's this about?* I wondered. The following week, over lunch, Wesley quickly got to the point. "A couple of years ago, when we were discussing America's many challenges and how Christians should respond, I think God was calling you to the nation, a ministry to address the nation. You need to seek God about this!" I sat stunned. *If this is inspired by God, it would be a dramatic change and an urgent call to action.*

At the time, I was content leading *Collegiate Impact*, a campus ministry I had started and led for years. Traveling from campus to campus, working with existing ministries, our rallying cry was to see hearts ignited and campuses transformed. And by God's grace, by delivering messages of repentance, holiness, and living in the "streams of living water" Jesus promised to all believers (John 7:37–39), we witnessed dramatic breakthroughs with the hearts of students set aflame for Christ. It was humbling to watch the presence of God bring students to tearful brokenness over personal sin, quickly followed by the joyful freedom of His forgiveness and fresh fillings of His Spirit. In turn, these students would go out on their campuses, touching the lives of others. However, Wesley was interrupting this dynamic season of ministry with an urgent exhortation to seek God about changing everything. My head was swirling.

A Turning Point

My wife and I began to seek God about the future, and in a matter of weeks, it became obvious that Wesley was right. As fulfilling as my years in campus ministry had been, it was time to marshal my convictions and zeal to start something new.

Unexpectedly, this turning point in our lives coincided with a turning point in America. It was 2013. The nation was already mired in spiritual darkness and widespread immorality, but America's dilemma was about to become far more serious. Troubling news headlines, pregnant with biblical implications, revealed that cultural seeds planted long ago were beginning to flourish.

Erosive Pluralism

It was only twelve years since the destruction wrought by Muslim terrorists on 9-11. Yet, Islam was growing in popularity and influence throughout our nation. Notwithstanding 2,977 lives lost and over 6,000 injured,[1] many remained naive to Islam's goal of world domination, which—at least behind closed mosque doors—called for replacing the U.S. Constitution with Sharia Law.[2] At the time, a Pew research study found that 85 to 90 percent of the 1.3 billion Muslims worldwide[3] rejected Islamic extremism, such as suicide bombings. Unfortunately, the balance of Muslims—some 195 million—supported extreme violence "often or sometimes."[4] Despite the warning signs, Americans continued to live with indifference to Islam's growing influence, as well as our nation's pluralistic atmosphere—an atmosphere that was increasingly rejecting the God of the Bible who had blessed us beyond measure.

Racial Divides

In 2013, Black Lives Matter (BLM), a Marxist political ruse disguised as a civil rights movement, emerged to present a fresh threat to national unity. In the wake of George Zimmerman's acquittal for killing Trayvon Martin in self-defense, BLM emerged to further incite racial tension. Meanwhile, President Barack Obama started his second term as the first ethnic minority to fill the Oval Office. While hope had soared four years earlier for new levels of racial harmony, Trayvon Martin's murder in 2012 and a surging BLM movement in 2013 made America as deeply divided as ever.[5]

Climate Fear

In 2013, the United Nations (UN) published what was hailed as the definitive report on global warming, supporting former Vice President Al Gore's assertion that the science was settled and, without dramatic changes, a global catastrophe was quickly approaching.[6] Even so, due to contradictory scientific data, many Americans were skeptical. The disconnect begged the question: Was the science settled, or was this yet another false alarm to advance the narrative of global problems necessitating global governance boards—such as the UN—to wield greater power?

A New Opiate

Already vulnerable, in 2013, for the first time, over half of Americans, 58 percent, believed that "getting high" should be legal.[7] Passing referendums to legalize recreational marijuana in late 2012, Colorado and Washington state were scrambling in 2013 to "set up regulatory schemes to safely and lawfully sell—and tax—recreational marijuana."[8] Eleven states quickly followed suit, with another 15 decriminalizing the recreational use of marijuana.[9]

Marriage Under Fire

On June 26, 2013, the U.S. Supreme Court ruled that the Defense of Marriage Act (DOMA) passed by Congress and signed into law by President Clinton in 1996 was unconstitutional. The ruling paved the way for the court's landmark *Obergefell vs. Hodges* decision, handed down two years later to the day, providing constitutional shelter for same-sex marriage. Just 16 years after Ellen came out on her popular sitcom, the gay community had earned the right to marry.

Big Brother

In 2013, the National Security Agency whistleblower Edward Snowden exposed the extent of the agency's intrusive classified national surveillance program. One news outlet warned, "The revelations were shocking: the scope and depth of the NSA's collection of private data stopped looking like a conspiracy theory and became a cold, hard reality we all had to face."[10] Soon, many Americans were asking, to what degree is the government storing information about us and why?

Religious Relapse

In 2013, Pew Research reported that an unprecedented "46 million Americans—one-fifth of the [adult] population—had no religious affiliation, the so-called 'nones.'"[11] The "nones" continued to grow throughout 2013 and beyond until eventually leveling off. Likewise, a later Gallop poll marked 2013 as the beginning of a steady decline in the importance of religious faith among Americans.[12]

And Now

This was the national landscape when Wesley and I met that memorable September day. Since 2013, I have felt it increasingly important to be ever-watchful and to filter current events through what I know to be true of God's dealings with nations.

Headlines with biblical implications continue to capture my attention. How many school teachers will resign or lose their jobs for not surrendering to LGBTQ advocacy? How long will gender fluidity replace the truth that God designed two distinct genders (Genesis 1:27; Matthew 19:4)? How many doctors will be penalized or threatened to lose their medical licenses for prescribing early, cheap, effective COVID-19 treatments or for speaking out against other misguided protocols? To what degree will our First Amendment right of free speech be subverted through weaponized disinformation accusations and biased social media platforms? If freedom of speech is restricted, how long until the government, with social media in tow, censors biblical truths, including Jesus being the only way to God? In the name of pandemic preparedness (and other global issues), to what degree does God expect individual nations to relinquish their sovereignty to international governance boards such as the World

Health Organization? Is God in agreement with our government's policy on open borders, allowing almost anyone and everyone to cross?

Most importantly, how long will Christians neglect to address these issues? Will we take the time to understand the biblical underpinnings of what is taking place? Will we come to understand the consequences of not contending for righteousness on every issue God speaks to? Ultimately, will the church not only forfeit its role as the conscience of the nation but also forgo its opportunity to influence culture for good?

Most sobering, if we refuse to follow biblical mandates now, how much longer can we expect the power and presence of God to rest upon us? Or, like Samson after his infamous haircut, has God's power and presence already departed?

The body of Christ needs to step up. But how?

The Need

Once my wife and I chose to follow God's call, He began to reveal the need of the hour. It is a need that any Christian can help meet—the need to live as forerunners.

A forerunner is someone who comes before someone or something else. Because a forerunner precedes something just around the corner, forerunners carry a timely message to their families, friends, churches, coworkers, communities, and nation. To discern a "now" message, biblical forerunners compared cultural realities to God's Word. They took steps to influence the culture toward godliness, or to at least consider godliness. They were uncompromising, even when facing great adversity. They warned the people of the consequences of living in defiance of God's will and ways. And, as much as God showed them about the future, they proclaimed what was coming. Put simply, a forerunner's contribution centers on understanding what is happening in culture from a biblical perspective, influencing those around them, discerning what is likely coming, and warning others.

Biblical Forerunners

Jesus was a forerunner in too many ways to count. He was a forerunner to the fullness of God's kingdom when He declared, "The kingdom of God is at hand" (Mark 1:15 ESV). At hand meant that God's kingdom had now arrived and, for the first time, was in reach of Jesus' listeners. It was a "now" message because it was time to become a citizen of God's kingdom through humbly confessing one's sin and believing in Jesus as the Son of God. Each day, as more and more people come to faith in Christ, we are getting closer to the fullness of God's kingdom on earth—what Jesus described as a tree that becomes the largest in a garden (Matthew 13:31–32). But even with the fulfillment of the Great Commission (Matthew 28:18–20), God's kingdom will not enter its ultimate fullness until the New Age begins (Revelation 21:1-22:5).

By teaching and training His disciples, Jesus was a forerunner to the launching of the church (Acts 2:1–47). Jesus is also our personal forerunner, being the first one to enter behind the veil, a place where each of us will one day follow (Hebrews 6:17–20). Jesus was His own forerunner, declaring that everyone who claims Him as Savior and Lord must prepare for His return (Matthew 24:1–25:46; Mark 13:1–37; Luke 21:5–36).

Amazing as Jesus' forerunner example is, for the purposes of *Called to Contend*, His forerunner messages to the seven churches in Asia

Minor are most important. In Revelation 2 and 3, Jesus calls five of these churches to repent of specific sins. What was about to come to each of those churches depended upon what these Christians did with His message.

The other two churches received very different warnings. The church at Smyrna was called to persevere because severe testing was coming (Revelation 2:8–11). The church in Philadelphia had passed the perseverance test but was exhorted to hold fast to Christ through coming difficulty so as not to lose their reward (Revelation 3:7–13).

Characteristic of any forerunner, Jesus talked about the future. His message was, and still is today, to get ready now because of what is coming. Like any forerunner should also do, Jesus compared the current state of affairs with His Father's will. Jesus then called churches to repent. What these churches chose to do with His message would affect their level of anointing, which would have numerous implications for those outside the church.

John the Baptist provides an equally compelling example for us to follow.

John

An angel announced to John's father, Zechariah, that he would grow up to be Jesus' forerunner:

> And it is he [John] who will go *as a forerunner* before Him [Jesus] in the spirit and power of Elijah, to turn the hearts of the fathers back to their children, and the disobedient to the attitude of the righteous, to make ready a people prepared for the Lord.
>
> Luke 1:17 NASB

John's ministry centered on calling people to repent to see families restored and lives changed to prepare for the Messiah's soon arrival (Luke 1:76–77). He compared the culture with God's will and called people to be baptized for the forgiveness of sins (Luke 3:1–3). By repeatedly confronting King Herod, he fearlessly called out the evil he observed in government (Mark 6:17–18). He also confronted the hypocrisy of the religious leaders (Luke 3:7–8, 18–20; Matthew 3:7). John not only gave breathtaking announcements of the Messiah's soon arrival but also warned the people of coming judgment:

> Even now the ax of God's judgment is poised, ready to sever the roots of the trees. Yes, every tree that does not produce good fruit will be chopped down and thrown into the fire ... But someone is coming soon who is greater than I am ... He is ready to separate the chaff from the wheat with his winnowing fork. Then he will clean up the threshing area, gathering the wheat into his barn but burning the chaff with never-ending fire.

Matthew 3:10–12

Modeled by John, addressing the future and its implications for the people, is central to a forerunner message.

Others

In addition to Jesus and John, many others lived as forerunners. As a preacher of righteousness, Noah became the first forerunner when he understood what was coming, built an ark, and "warned the world of God's righteous judgment" (2 Peter 2:5; Genesis 6:13–22; Hebrews 11:7). Moses, having received a "now" message from God, understood the hearts of the people, saw what was coming, and composed a lament of warning in his farewell address to the nation (Deuteronomy 31:16–19; 32:1–47).

Jeremiah proclaimed God's "now" message, urging everyone to repent before devastation came to Israel (Jeremiah 3:11–14; 11:1–17). Understanding that the Jews were to be annihilated within months, Queen Esther called the Jews in Susa, the Persian capital city, to fast for three days for God to show them mercy (Esther 4:15–16). The apostle Peter strongly urged thousands at Pentecost to "Save yourselves from this crooked generation!" (Acts 2:40). Why did they need to save themselves? Because God's judgment of humanity is on heaven's calendar. The warning to prepare for this coming judgment is as relevant today as it was in Peter's day.

What, then, is the need of the hour? It is to be forerunners who see what is taking place in the present, understand what the future likely holds, and do something about it. Not everyone is called to influence multitudes of people like Jesus, John the Baptist, and other biblical forerunners. But our calling is no less important.

God's call for us is to influence as many family members, friends, neighbors, and coworkers as possible. All of us can compare what is taking place around us with God's character and commands. Each of us can be a godly example and influence others. All of us are called to stand firm in the face of wickedness. Each of us can warn others of the consequences of living in defiance to God's will and ways. All of us can be forerunners.

Forecasting the Future

As forerunners to what is coming, we must speak in terms of what is *likely* ahead. We cannot speak dogmatically about the future because

God has not told us everything. Indeed, His outcomes are not as certain as we might think, and many times the future is conditional.

We know how the crisis in Esther's day came out, but it was not that way at the moment. Esther did not say, "Fast! God will hear our prayers and genocide will be averted!" Instead, Esther called the Jews to fast, and before approaching the king, she surrendered to God's will, stating, "If I die, I die" (Esther 4:16). In response to their fasting and Esther's humble courage, God used Esther to save the day. As forerunners, we must discern what is taking place and declare what the future *likely* holds. Nothing more. Nothing less.

The biblical prophets called out the sins of the people and warned everyone of coming judgment. However, on some occasions, the people humbled themselves with genuine repentance and averted judgment. Other times, God's judgment was delayed. Examples include the delay of Judah's judgment under Josiah's leadership and the averting of the destruction of Assyria's capital city, Nineveh (2 Kings 22:14–20; Jonah 3:1–10). Therefore, we must declare the forerunner message God has given us by calling people to seek Him in the present, not making hard and fast promises about the future.

Becoming Influencers

Like each of the forerunners highlighted, we need to hear from God about the day and hour we are living, as well as gain His perspective on what the future likely holds. Noah and Jeremiah heard from God directly. Esther was informed by her servants and older cousin, Mordecai, of what was coming (Esther 4:1–8).

John the Baptist likely grasped his "now" message and forerunner role through his parents and Jesus' mother (Luke 1:5–80). He would also have gained insight about himself and the coming Messiah through the written Word of God (Isaiah 7:14; 40:3–5; 61:1–2; Micah 5:2; Malachi 3:1). Further, John sought God throughout his adult life in the desert, which no doubt brought clarity to his calling and deeper conviction to speak God's Word in power (Luke 1:80).

To develop a forerunner message, Jesus also teaches us to rely upon the Holy Spirit:

> When the Spirit of truth comes, he will guide you into all truth. He will not speak on his own but will tell you what he has heard. He will tell you about the future. He will bring me glory by telling you whatever he receives from me.
>
> John 16:13–14

Relying upon the written Word of God and the Holy Spirit is a powerful combination to be embraced by all Christians and is essential to becoming a forerunner.

Our Response

Be assured that God is already revealing the signs of the times in our day, just as Jesus exhorted the crowds to understand in His day (Luke 12:54–56). God is revealing His "now" message to us! We must ask: Based on what God is revealing to me in Scripture and in culture, what is likely coming? Then ask: Lord, what do you want me to do? Who do you want me to tell?

We must follow the example of Jesus, John the Baptist, and other godly forerunners so that we, too, can influence our families, friends, churches, and communities. Like them and so many others, we must not retreat, but courageously contend for the faith. This is what was required of them. No less will be required of us today.

• • •

We are living in unusual days—days contested between profound good and shocking evil. It is to the nature of this battle that we must turn our attention to next.

PART 1
What's Going On?

THE BATTLE OF THE AGES

You should know this, Timothy, that in the last days there will be very difficult times. For people will love only themselves and their money. They will be boastful and proud, scoffing at God, disobedient to their parents, and ungrateful. They will consider nothing sacred. They will be unloving and unforgiving; they will slander others and have no self-control. They will be cruel and hate what is good. They will betray their friends, be reckless, be puffed up with pride, and love pleasure rather than God. They will act religious, but they will reject the power that could make them godly. Stay away from people like that!

2 Timothy 3:1–5

Today, we see Paul's vivid description of the last days unfolding. Paul also wrote, "Now the Holy Spirit tells us clearly that in the last days some will turn away from the true faith; they will follow deceptive spirits and teachings that come from demons" (1 Timothy 4:1).

High-profile Christians continue to leave the faith. Bestselling author and megachurch pastor Joshua Harris stated, "I have undergone a massive shift in regard to my faith in Jesus … By all the measurements

I have for defining a Christian, I am not a Christian."[1] Former *Desiring God* website contributor, Paul Maxwell, shared, "I think it's important to say that I'm just not a Christian anymore, and it feels really good."[2]

Others have sent shockwaves throughout Christendom, renouncing the faith they once promoted, such as mega-podcasters Rhett and Link and Hillsong songwriter Marty Sampson.[3] Sadly, more will follow. Perhaps you know people who once walked with God, only to "turn away from the true faith" and "follow deceptive spirits" and "teachings that come from demons." Turning away from Jesus can happen without spiritual interference, but Paul highlights in the last days, demonic activity will increasingly be at play.

Based on Paul's description of culture before Jesus returns, increasing evil, and those brazenly leaving the faith, it appears that the battle of the ages is upon us. Throughout history God's kingdom has advanced and the domain of darkness has counterattacked. But I believe what we are facing now will continue to escalate until Jesus returns. Buckle up. No civilization has experienced what is currently coming upon the earth.

Nature of the Battle

This battle is an ever-increasing conflict in the unseen realm. Satan and his minions are pitted against God and His angelic armies. This battle also takes place in the physical realm. These realms are inseparable and, thankfully, God has equipped us with His Word, His Spirit, and the body of Christ to navigate it.

To see this battle as primarily cultural or political is to miss its spiritual underpinnings—a critical liability in and of itself. Further, we will likely underestimate the dangers we are confronting. Namely, the lies and deceptions of the one who "comes only to steal, kill, and destroy" (John 10:10 NASB). This is the one whom Peter warned seeks to devour Christians like a ferocious lion (1 Peter 5:8). This is serious.

The Gospel is Central

Central to this conflict is to see people repent of their sins and believe in Jesus as Savior and Lord. These who come to faith are transferred from the domain of darkness to God's kingdom (Colossians 1:13). Jesus states when calling Paul to faith and enlisting him into the battle:

> Get up and stand on your feet; for this purpose I [Jesus] have appeared to you, to appoint you a minister and a witness not only to the things which you have seen, but also to the things in which I will appear to you; rescuing you from the Jewish people and from the Gentiles, to whom I am sending you, to open their eyes so that they may turn from darkness to light and from the dominion of Satan to God, that they may receive forgiveness of sins and an inheritance among those who have been sanctified by faith in Me. "So, King Agrippa, I did not prove disobedient to the heavenly vision, but kept declaring ... that they should repent and turn to God, performing deeds appropriate to repentance."
>
> Acts 26:16–20 NASB

Notice, Jesus highlights the spiritual war at play alongside the practical steps of faith, forgiveness, and repentance. Specifically, He emphasizes light versus darkness, Satan's dominion versus God's, and the souls of men. This is a battle that has been fought throughout history—a battle that will likely come to its conclusion in our generation.

Only Culture Wars?

Culture is made up of the choices of individuals. Continuously, each person chooses good or evil, right or wrong, godliness or wickedness. Collective choices made by churches, communities, and nations also matter. They matter in the moment, and they matter for eternity because our choices have consequences. God and Satan know this. To dismiss what the Bible identifies as dangerous cultural lies and wickedness as irrelevant culture wars is fatal.

How do these lies brainwash broader culture and even infiltrate our churches? Typically, the delivery vehicles are mainstream media, politicians, the entertainment industry, and public education. Neglecting to guard our spiritual gates in each of these domains has only created confusion and chaos—something our spiritual adversary is delighted to capitalize upon.

In America, we are witnessing unprecedented levels of sexual perversion, child and adult homicide, divorce, adultery, racial hatred, censorship, the killing of the unborn, suicidal ideation, same-sex marriage, gender dysphoria, pedophilia, polyamory, political corruption, opiate addiction, and all manner of egregious behaviors.

To understand what is going on, we must replace the erroneous term *culture war* with the biblically accurate term *spiritual war*. Understanding this critical distinction enables us to see what is taking place from God's perspective.

Complacency or Engagement

C.S. Lewis, Oxford University professor and reluctant convert to Christianity, wrote, "There is no neutral ground in the universe. Every square inch, every split second is claimed by God, and counterclaimed by Satan."[4] Nonetheless, American Christians are typically unaware or indifferent to this spiritual conflict. This is true for numerous reasons, but I will highlight one.

Theological Excuses

A common declaration among Christians, as society continues its moral freefall, is, "But we know who wins in the end!" This statement implies that we are secure in our eternal destiny, and nothing is truly at stake now. Thus, we can relax and indulge our sedentary lifestyles. Let's get back to surfing the internet, shopping, vacationing, scrolling social media, watching movies, playing video games, and the like because we know who wins in the end. Really? This is our best response?

Yes, God wins. But we cannot afford to sit around waiting for the happy ending. At present, much is at stake in our families and communities. We must not live disobedient lives by ignoring Jesus' mandate to influence those around us, all the while handing over the next generation to every form of depravity. Until we see Jesus returning on the clouds, all Christians are called to stand firm in righteousness, as well as expose evil (Ephesians 5:11–16).

Similarly, we hear the alarming news of escalating evil and simplistically declare, "Well, God is sovereign." Again, implied is the idea that our eternal destiny is secure and all the rising evil around us is simply part of God's unfolding plan. Therefore, we believe that we have a theological license to say and do nothing. After all, if God wanted things to change, He is sovereign and would change them. Regrettably, we have missed the Scriptural theme that God has already sovereignly called every Christian to contend for the faith—privately and publicly.

Because we know who wins in the end, we should be compelled to fight wickedness. Because God is sovereign, we should grab five smooth stones and run to the hottest part of the battle. Because God is sovereign, we should turn-off the TV, put on the full armor of God, and contend for the faith (Ephesians 6:10–17).

How Did We Get Here?

How did America undergo such a rapid transformation from some degree of decency in many families and communities to utter moral chaos? Typically, we view Satan as an occasional nemesis who only comes around now and then to tempt individuals. The Bible challenges this understanding.

Jesus exposed Satan's widespread influence when He stated, "The prince of this world is coming" (John 14:30 NIV). Satan himself stated that he has dominion over "all the kingdoms of the world" (Matthew 4:8). Paul described him as the "prince of the power of the air" and "the god of this world" (Ephesians 2:2; 2 Corinthians 4:4). The apostle John wrote that "the whole earth is under the power of the evil one" (1 John 5:19). John describes the dragon (Satan) summoning a great terrifying beast whose influence will encompass the entire earth, crush it, and wear down the saints before Jesus' return (Revelation 13:1–10, Daniel 7:19–25). In brief, the evil one's scope and influence is well beyond what most American Christians have considered.

Global Ambition

John saw Satan chained and thrown into the bottomless pit for a thousand years "so that he would *no longer deceive the nations*" (Revelation 20:1–3, emphasis added). Since this prophecy has not yet been fulfilled, we currently live in the era when Satan's activity to deceive entire nations is at play.

John further explains that at the end of Jesus' millennial reign, Satan will be released to roam the earth to deceive nations again. This time, he deceives Gog and Magog, which in turn deceives other nations, creating an evil coalition "as large as the sand of the seashore" (Revelation 20:7–9). Once all of Scripture is considered, we see that Satan's strategy often begins with individuals (Acts 5:3; 1 Peter 5:8), but his endgame is to deceive entire nations and the world (Revelation 12:9).

Grasping the spiritual nature of the battle before us and Satan's widespread ambitions, we must address these questions: Are there recent examples of Satan influencing entire nations? How is Satan influencing America?

Nations Deceived

An overview of the last hundred years reveals an adversary who is alive and quite active. The following leaders were capable of carrying out great evil without the help of Satan and his minions. Yet, as one gets acquainted with biblical principles and historical accounts, Satan's fingerprints are everywhere.

Russia (Soviet Union)

The Marxist deception, developed and popularized by Karl Marx (1818–1883) and further adapted by Vladimir Lenin (1870–1924) and Joseph Stalin (1878–1953), led to the death of more than twenty million Russians. That's not a typo, nor is it Russia's wartime casualties, but the massacre of their own people.[5] What madness was this?

Built on totalitarianism—the ideology that the government must control both how people behave and what they think—anyone who publicly disagreed with the government, even to the smallest degree, meant imprisonment or death. The millions of fatalities were due to purges of dissidents, such as the Red Terror and Great Terror purges, politically orchestrated famines, mass executions, forced migrations, and Gulag cruelty.[6]

After surviving this nightmare, political dissident and Orthodox Christian Aleksandr Solzhenitsyn championed the biblical theme of walking in the truth by urging his countrymen to "Live not by lies!" (John 17:15–19; Ephesians 4:25; 3 John 3–4).[7] Solzhenitsyn believed that Russia's Marxist political culture of deceit and unspeakable evil was fundamentally a spiritual conflict between good versus evil.[8]

Historian David Satter agrees, stating, "For the first time, a state was created that was based explicitly on atheism and claimed infallibility. This was totally incompatible with Western civilization, which presumes the existence of a higher power over and above society and the state."[9]

Stalin offered another glimpse into this sinister regime when he brazenly remarked, "I consider it completely unimportant who in the party will vote, or how, but what is extraordinarily important is this—who will count the votes, and how."[10] Fearmongering, creating a culture of lies, and rigging elections are among Satan's primary strategies that result in nationwide death and destruction.

Nazi Germany

Coordinating media, literature, visual arts, filmmaking, theater, music, and broadcasting, Germany's *Ministry of Enlightenment and Propaganda* vigorously enforced an Arian race superiority myth. Led by Joseph Goebbels, this agency deceived the people by means of lies and clandestine maneuvering to advance Hitler's goals. In the end, six million Jews were murdered, while millions of others died during Germany's pursuit to rule the world. The evil one routinely positions leadership to promote propaganda through the mainstream media and the arts to deceive entire nations.

Cambodia

Deceived by Marxist tenets that promote violence and division through class warfare, Cambodia's Khmer Rouge were responsible for the death of 2.5 million of their own people, 1970–1975. Key to the enemy's aims are divide-and-conquer strategies that stir up hostility between the rich and poor, one race against another, and those with progressive values against those with traditional values.

European Socialism

In recent decades, Europeans have come to believe that a softer version of Marxism is the answer. Based upon Socialism's subtle, deceptive conditioning to get the people to rely on government rather than God, evangelical Christians comprise only two to three percent of Europe's population.[11] With promises of universal health care, saving lives through climate change policy, and the humanistic state educating children and youth, people learn to trust the state to meet every need. All this and more requires massive government, which results in societal control. Satan has duped Europeans with a shrewdly attractive version of totalitarianism to achieve his goal of blinding the lost from coming to faith (2 Corinthians 4:3–4).

Uganda

Ugandan Christians recount how dark spiritual forces brought devastation to their country in the 70s and 80s through witchcraft, paganism, and the sinister leadership of Idi Amin (1925–2003) and Milton Obeta (1925–2005). These dictators, ruling 1971 to 1985, killed their political opposition and Christians alike.

Only through repentance and deep intercession, followed by a long season of revival in the church and a broad spiritual awakening throughout the nation, did Uganda change. As God drew near, cultural dynamics improved—even miraculously! Due to Christian influence, the government created a Department of Ethics and Integrity. Today, Ugandans describe what happened—both the widespread destruction and the following national blessings—as fundamentally spiritual.[12]

Secular historians can only provide human explanations for the widespread killing and cultural devastation that overwhelmed each of these nations. However, Scripture provides a deeper principle: the distancing of God through the rejection of His will and ways creates a spiritual vacuum—a vacuum that the evil one anxiously waits to fill (2 Chronicles 15:1–2; James 4:7–10; Revelation 20:3).

Recruiting

How does Satan recruit human accomplices, many of whom have no idea they are pawns in this spiritual war? How is the adversary so effective at deceiving entire nations?

Jesus identified Satan as "a murderer from the beginning," with goals to "steal, kill, and destroy" (John 8:44; 10:10). And his desire is to do so on a broad scale.

Jesus also gave Satan a title unique in Scripture: the father of lies (John 8:44). Reflected in these nations, the adversary cannot win in a fair exchange of ideas. Therefore, his primary strategy is to lie and deceive with false narratives aimed at changing cultural mindsets. Cultural mindsets are also known as the *spirit of the age* or *zeitgeist*. In other words, Satan uses lies to shape public opinion to destroy nations.

With so many spiritually lost people, why doesn't he simply use them with more forthright intentions? Why does he resort to this complex strategy of creating a culture of lies? Even people who hate God and Jesus Christ rarely want to destroy themselves, their nation, or civilization. In other words, Satan's goals are far more malevolent than what non-Christians typically want to pursue. So, he must use widespread deception to create a culture of lies.

Given these dynamics and that the deception of entire nations is a key aspect of the escalating battle, we must heed Paul's warning:

> For we are not fighting against flesh-and-blood enemies, but against evil rulers and authorities of the unseen world, against mighty powers in this dark world, and against evil spirits in the heavenly places.
>
> Ephesians 6:12

What About America?

A perfect storm of deception has aggressively infiltrated America: algorithms programmed toward predetermined ends, mainstream media spinning news stories, social media censorship, biased fact-checkers, attacks on those who speak the truth, cancel culture intimidation, citizens bombarded with lies until lies become the "truth," the fabrication of false narratives, and the unquestioned acceptance of leaders who claim to be following the science and data.

This perfect storm gets worse. Anyone who chooses to speak against the dominant narrative is accused of spreading misinformation, disinformation, or malinformation—information that stems from the truth but is judged inaccurate due to exaggeration. Those who criticize the narrative are accused of promoting hate or believing in conspiracy theories. Welcome to America, where each of these forms of deception and bullying are on full display.

What are the consequences of neglecting to address the lies at the root of the spiritual battle all around us? What happens when we do not find our voice on key issues, and the evil one, full of lies and deception, does?

Let's answer these questions using America's response to the COVID-19 pandemic (2020–2023). The COVID-19 virus is real and has caused numerous deaths, but "the father of lies" found a way to leverage this crisis for his ends.

Immobilized by Fear

Wuhan, China's late 2019 outbreak of the COVID-19 virus, quickly spread worldwide, becoming fertile soil for lies and deception. Yet again, misguided and sinful people are capable of what you are about to read. But upon taking a closer look, we can discern dark spiritual forces pushing the pandemic toward evil outcomes, which became one of the most bizarre seasons in American history.

Data showed that those who succumbed to COVID were heavily weighted toward the elderly and those with pre-existing health conditions. However, because of the daily media bombardment of new cases and a climbing death toll, Americans feared testing positive was a death sentence. Suddenly, fear spread nationwide, surprisingly, even among Christians who claim to believe in eternal life.

Silencing Truth

The Centers for Disease and Control (CDC) reported the COVID recovery rate in 2020, and confirmed thereafter, between 99.4 and 99.7%.[13] In 2020, eighty-eight percent of New York COVID fatalities were found to have two or more comorbidities. Remarkably, in late August 2020, seven months after the COVID outbreak in the U.S., "The CDC published data showing only six percent of the total death count had COVID-19 listed as the sole cause of death."[14]

Since these facts were seldom reported, healthy Americans continued to live in fear while health authorities and political leaders persistently advised lockdowns—initially only to be implemented for "two weeks to slow the spread." Even while top epidemiologists warned against this approach, some of the loudest contrary voices, claiming to be following the science and the data, prevailed. In the end, data proved that states that implemented strict lockdowns fared no better than states that did not.[15] Yet, the pandemic of fear, with its disproportionate public policies, continued.

Culture of Lies

Addressing COVID-19, Psychiatrist Dr. Mark McDonald stated, "There is a delusional psychosis that has taken over where people are impervious to rational thinking…They are psychotically managed by their fear."[16] Tragically, when we operate out of fear, we become more susceptible to the father of lies.

Jeffrey Tucker is the founder of the Brownstone Institute, an organization that drew upon top scholarship to find the truth regarding the COVID pandemic. In *To Be Ruled by Liars*, Tucker summarizes the first three years of the pandemic:

> Major swaths of the leaders of our public culture—in government, media, and industry—have been lying to us ... We know now what we once suspected but lacked confirmation: the loss of liberty in our times is rooted in core claims that have proven to be untrue... We are indeed exhausted by the lies. We are also exhausted from learning the truth about the lies because, of course, the elites deny ever having lied in the first place.[17]

Undermining Experts

Dr. Martin Kulldorff was a Harvard University professor during the first two years of the pandemic and helped write the *Great Barrington Declaration*. The purpose of this declaration was to correct America's bizarre COVID response. The declaration contradicted the COVID lockdown guidance provided by infectious disease expert and presidential advisor Dr. Anthony Fauci. Kulldorff explained that his declaration was nothing new:

> It's just the basic fundamental principles of public health that existed in the pandemic preparedness plan that was prepared many years before [the COVID-19 outbreak]. It's sort of astonishing that it wasn't followed from the very beginning of the pandemic.[18]

In a baffling response, National Institute of Health Director Dr. Francis Collins emailed Dr. Fauci and referred to Kulldorff and the other *Barrington Declaration* authors from Stanford University and Oxford

University as "fringe scientists." Soon, Dr. Kulldorff was attacked on mainstream media by Dr. Collins, Dr. Fauci, and others. When asked if he had ever considered himself to be a "fringe epidemiologist," Kulldorff said, "No, I have not, but I guess, when the public health leaders get it wrong, then it's an honor to be a fringe epidemiologist."[19]

As he continued to be maligned for supposedly spreading disinformation, others defended the declaration's scientific accuracy and Dr. Kulldorff's reputation:

> Dr. Kulldorff is one of the most qualified public health pandemic experts in the United States... As a prominent epidemiologist and statistician, Kulldorff has worked on detecting and monitoring infectious disease outbreaks for two decades. His methods are widely used around the world and by almost every state health department in the United States.[20]

And yet louder voices, ignoring what had been successfully accomplished during previous pandemics, dominated the media.

More than 63,000 medical professionals and scientists signed *The Great Barrington Declaration*, calling for an immediate change in America's COVID response.[21] Yet, to this day, most Americans—including Christians—have not heard of the *Great Barrington Declaration*.

This is how the father of lies works—he creates false narratives that are promoted through a culture of lies and impedes people from finding the truth. He silences, intimidates, and suppresses any and all competing voices.

Tailored Deception

When deceiving nations, the father of lies tailors his strategies. Muslim countries have their own version of totalitarianism, centered on a culture of fear, the infidel narrative, and Sharia Law. Some nations are deceived by paganism, drawing on spiritual power through rituals and incantations, as well as trying to appease spirits through offerings and sacrifices. Others are blinded by widespread hedonism, humanism, and naturalism.

Deception American Style

In 1948, Romanian Pastor Richard Wurmbrand was imprisoned for his faith. After years of unspeakable torture, he and his fellow prisoners were forced to listen to messages over loudspeakers from 5:00 a.m. to 10:00 p.m., repeating, "Communism is good," "Christianity is dead," "Your wife has left you," and "No one loves you." Each of these messages and more were intended to break their will, brainwash, and convert them to Marxism. Although the sessions of physical torture were horrific, Wurmbrand described this continual psychological warfare while being drugged as the most difficult to endure.

Released in 1965, Wurmbrand and his wife eventually settled in America and started a ministry for persecuted Christians, *The Voice of the Martyrs*. Enjoying American freedom and ministering internationally, the Wurmbrands came to realize that, while communist brainwashing was forced, Americans voluntarily succumb to the father of lies. Numbed by radio, TV, and materialistic lifestyles, they observed that most Americans lacked discernment, with only a scant few genuinely interested in God and eternal things. They concluded that America's deception, though in stark contrast to communist prisons, was equally dangerous.[22]

Our Response

America is in a spiritual war between good and evil, truth versus lies, and righteousness versus wickedness, namely, God versus Satan. It is a spiritual war, but one that is played out daily in the physical realm.

As the battle of the ages escalates, discerning truth and the lies of the enemy will not get easier. Regarding this battle, Jesus' first warning is, "Don't let anyone mislead you" (Mark 13:5). Guaranteed, by Jesus, a deceptive culture of lies will continue to escalate until He returns.

Thankfully, Jesus told us how to discern good from evil. He tells us to be on the lookout for those who appear harmless but are as dangerous as wolves. He tells us to examine the fruit of a person's life and ministry (Matthew 7:15–18). Jesus assures us that we can rely on the Holy Spirit because He is "the Spirit of Truth" who will "guide you into all truth" (John 14:17; 16:13). Jesus also modeled how to use Scripture when confronted with Satan's temptations (Matthew 4:1–11).

Because the battle of the ages has arrived, applying Jesus' instructions has never been more important. Whether we become casualties or conquerors is up to us.

• • •

Satan is actively seeking to deceive nations—including America. If Satan's endgame is to deceive nations, it is crucial we understand what God thinks about nations. This, too, will inform our "now" message. It is to this topic we must turn our attention to next.

NATIONS MATTER

For by his great power he rules forever.
He watches every movement of the nations.

Psalm 66:7

During his 1991 State of the Union Address, President George H.W. Bush (1924–2018) called for a "New World Order." Bush described his vision for "open borders, open trade, and … open minds," and this New World Order as "a big idea where diverse nations are drawn together in common cause to achieve the universal aspirations of mankind."[1] A few months prior, speaking at the UN, he highlighted the need for strong international alliances and lauded the UN for "fulfilling its promise as the world's parliament of peace."[2] For the first time, repeatedly and publicly, the most powerful head of state earnestly advocated globalism at the expense of individual sovereign nations. To Bush, it was part of a brave new world.

Globalism Today

Fast forward thirty years, we observe this economic, political, environmental, global approach to governing humanity taking on a life of its own. Many of the most influential leaders in business and government now openly promote some version of globalism.

During the last of three 2022 Asia-Pacific Economic Cooperation (APEC) summits, French President Emmanuel Macron called these nations to join "a single world order."[3] That same year, the founder of the World Economic Forum, Klaus Schwab, stated to his annual assembly of global influencers, "The future is not just happening. The future is built by us—by a powerful community, as you here in this room."[4] If an assembly of mostly unelected power brokers exercising their coordinated influence to shape the planet's destiny sounds a bit creepy, it should, as should the moniker "New World Order."

Schwab is also known for publishing his global predictions, architecture for a New World Order, and wish-list in his popular book, *COVID-19: The Great Reset*. He sees the interdependence of nations as superior to individual sovereign nations and advocates a version of globalism characterized by the oversight of all of humanity, including data collection and surveillance of each person. Distasteful to many, surveillance measures are sold with a smile by highlighting their ability to curb future pandemics.[5]

According to Schwab's global reset, it is the responsibility of corporations to inject themselves into moral issues and the well-being of humanity through Environmental, Social, and Governance (ESG) initiatives.[6] The social aspect includes corporations addressing diversity, equity, and inclusion (DEI). Of course, this means the advocacy of what is often understood as special rights for gays, transgenders, women, people of color, and everyone but white heterosexual men. ESG values made popular in 2004, have "grown from a corporate social responsibility initiative launched by the United Nations into a global phenomenon representing more than $30 trillion in assets under management."[7] Thus, far-reaching ESG is providing guidelines for businesses to follow, which addresses everything from climate change policies to the mainstreaming of LGBTQ lifestyles.

Further, Schwab grooms the best and brightest to take influential leadership positions through his Forum of Young Global Leaders program. Among the most notable graduates are former Prime Minister of the United Kingdom, Tony Blair; Prime Minister of Canada, Justin Trudeau; former Chancellor of Germany, Angela Merkel; co-founder of Google, Larry Page; co-founder of Facebook, Mark Zuckerberg, and Bill Gates, the ubiquitous founder of Microsoft.[8]

Throughout history, leaders boldly moved to conquer the world through military conquest. Genghis Khan, Attila the Hun, Alexander the Great, and Adolph Hitler come to mind. To modern globalists, nations maintain their name, sometimes elections, and a small degree of sovereignty. However, any meaningful decision-making is increasingly abdicated to international committees and governing boards, which are conveniently aloof from scrutiny or accountability.

Looks Good

To a globalist, only the coordinated efforts of international governance boards can effectively address the world's problems. These include groups such as the G-20 (group of 20 nations with the largest economies); G-7 (the integration of the Canadian, French, German, Italian, Japanese, Great Britain, and American governments); the WHO (global health policy influenced through the UN's World Health Organization); BRICS (an intergovernmental organization originally comprised of Brazil, Russia, India, China, and South Africa, which accepted five additional nations in 2024). Also, nations may become members of international accords such as the 2016 Paris Agreement, in which 194 nations permanently bound themselves together to stop global warming.[9] Globalists believe that independent nations making their own, presumably self-serving, decisions will ultimately cripple the planet.

In the aftermath of World War I, global peace became the impetus for creating the League of Nations, which is now understood as "The template for modern global governance."[10] The promise was clear: if humanity could discard sovereign nations with their irritating nationalistic spirit, war would become obsolete. After the failure of the League of Nations—World War II exposed the League's ineffectiveness—the United Nations picked up the mantle as an intergovernmental organization whose stated purposes are to "maintain international peace and security" and to solve "international problems of an economic, social, cultural, or humanitarian character."[11]

In the 1970s, overpopulation and pollution became global headline threats, with pollution eventually morphing into climate change alarm. Additional impetus to pursue global solutions is found in gender and racial inequalities, as well potential global economic downturns. Most recent and persuasive, because of humanity's fear of death, each nation must become synchronized with the global community for effective pandemic responses.

To a globalist, global problems require global solutions, which will only be effective if a small group of leaders provide supervision over the nations. This might sound quite enlightening, but the Bible teaches that God's plan for humanity is the opposite.

God Weighs-In

An ancient biblical genealogy known as *The Table of Nations* or *Origines Gentium* clarifies that individual sovereign nations were God's idea. Recounting Noah's family tree within a few generations of the flood, this genealogy states, "These are the families of the sons of Noah, according to their descendants, by their nations; and out of these the nations were separated on the earth after the flood" (Genesis 10:32 NASB). Here, we have the first reference of God's plan to create individual nations.

Through Moses, we learn that God alone assigns nations their location and appoints angelic supervision over each one:

> When the Most High assigned lands to the nations, when he divided up the human race, he established the boundaries of the peoples according to the number in his heavenly court.
>
> Deuteronomy 32:8

Understanding that nations are God's idea, we should probably push the pause button before replacing individual sovereign nations with globalism.

Nations Today

Do any New Testament writers either nullify or affirm God's design of separate sovereign nations? Or were nations simply an Old Testament reality? After all, God's initiatives of the Great Commission, proliferating churches in every tribe and language, and seeing His kingdom expand everywhere are global.

Even so, the apostle Paul affirms that God created nations, and that individual nations will continue to be birthed or removed at His discretion:

> From one man he [God] created all the nations throughout the whole earth. He decided beforehand when they should rise and fall, and he determined their boundaries.
>
> Acts 17:26

Not only does Paul assert that God created each nation, but He decides their boundaries and the duration of their existence. Secular historians will attribute a nation's borders to treaties, wars, and topography. However, Paul explains that God is behind it all.

In America's case, there is a divine purpose for its beginning in 1776, as well as positioning it to the north of Mexico, south of Canada, and having oceans bordering the east and west coasts. The same is true for every nation on earth—each one is sovereignly and strategically placed by God for His purposes. But what are His purposes for creating individual sovereign nations?

Restraining Evil

Separate nations impede wickedness. Before the flood, God regretted that He had created civilization because the earth became "filled with violence" with hearts of men and women plunging into utter depravity (Genesis 6:11–13). Post-flood, God separated the people into nations (Genesis 10:1–32), yet humanity again defied God, uniting to build the infamous tower of Babel to reach into heaven. This undertaking was a rejection of God's purpose for humanity to be "scattered over the face of the earth" (Genesis 11:1–9). Pride and the evil ambition to become God-like overtook civilization, a pattern that still haunts us today.

Yet, instead of sending another global catastrophe, God restrained the proliferation of evil by creating distinct languages to further separate each nation. Regardless of the degree to which mankind's current attempt at globalism is successful, the Bible teaches that it will ultimately fare no better than humanity's first attempt at Babel.

Eerily, the European Union's parliament building was intentionally modeled after a 1563 painting of the Tower of Babel. The inscription states, "Many tongues, one voice."[12] It was understood by the members of parliament that "The purpose of the European Union was to finish what Nimrud and the people together had failed to do some 3,500 years ago."[13]

Populating Heaven

Paul also asserts that God created individual nations to populate heaven:

> From one man he [God] created all the nations throughout the whole earth. He decided beforehand when they should rise and fall, and he determined their boundaries. *His purpose was for the nations to seek after God and perhaps feel their way toward him and find him*—though he is not far from any one of us.
>
> Acts 17:26–27 (emphasis added)

In other words, God uses the existence of separate nations to prepare the hearts of people to hear the gospel. What do individual sovereign nations have to do with more people coming to faith in Jesus? First, conflict between nations shakes people out of their lethargy. We see this at play when the prophet Azariah spoke to King Asa:

> For a long time Israel was without the true God, without a priest to teach them, and without the Law to instruct them. But whenever they were in trouble and turned to the Lord, the God of Israel, and sought him out, they found him. During those dark times, it was not safe to travel. Problems troubled the people of every land.

Nation fought against nation, and city against city, for God was troubling them with every kind of problem.

2 Chronicles 15:3–6

Once Asa understood God's purpose behind national problems and distresses, he boldly led the nation into repentance and the people "earnestly sought after God, and they found him." Joyfully, "The Lord gave them rest from their enemies on every side" (2 Chronicles 15:7–15).

The same dynamics have been at play throughout America's history. When a nation troubles America, Americans get trouble. And troubled people seek God.

During the Vietnam War (1955–75), 58,000 American soldiers lost their lives. Yet, God used this tragic time, along with the tumultuous drug culture and sexual revolution, to trouble Americans "with every kind of problem." These distresses ultimately stirred vast numbers of people to seek the answers to life and many found Jesus. The late 1960s through the mid-70s, an era known as the Jesus Revolution, was the last time America experienced a prolonged, massive harvest of souls.

God also populates heaven by blessing a nation, which stirs curiosity in other nations. After hearing of Solomon's wisdom and seeing for herself Israel's prosperity, the Queen of Sheba said:

> I didn't believe what was said until I arrived here and saw it with my own eyes. In fact, I had not heard the half of it! Your wisdom and prosperity are far beyond what I was told… Praise the Lord your God, who delights in you and has placed you on the throne of Israel. Because of the Lord's eternal love for Israel, he has made you king so you can rule with justice and righteousness.

1 Kings 10:7 & 9

Similarly, during my missionary journeys to Latvia, Thailand, Albania, China, and the Philippines, people were intrigued by our teams because of America's reputation as the greatest nation on earth. It was often easy to find an attentive audience to talk about Jesus as the Son of God and Savior of the world because people wanted to know what Americans believed.

God forms separate sovereign nations to impede wickedness and to create an environment where more people come to faith.

Divine Interaction

Not only does God create nations, but He interacts with each nation. When leaders of nations scheme against God, God laughs at them and rebukes them in His anger, as well as calls them to turn from evil (Psalm 2:1–12). God also rules each nation fairly, disciplines nations, and removes them (Psalm 9:5–8). God intervenes to humble nations, reminding them that they are comprised of mere mortals, and blesses nations that honor Him (Psalms 9:19–20; 33:12). God oversees nations:

> For by his great power he rules forever. He watches every movement of the nations.
>
> Psalm 66:7
>
> Because God judges and guides nations, the people rejoice: May the nations be glad and sing for joy; For You will judge the peoples with fairness and guide the nations on the earth.
>
> Psalm 67:4 NIV

A Beginning Without End

Often overlooked, after Jesus returns, individual nations will continue to exist as part of God's unfolding plan. Jesus will rule and reign from Jerusalem, the earth's capital city, where He will literally be the King of Kings (Revelation 19:16)! The prophet Micah gives us a look into the activity of nations during Jesus' millennial reign:

> In the last days, the mountain of the Lord's house will be the highest of all—the most important place on earth. It will be raised above the other hills, and people from all over the world will stream there to worship. People from many nations will come and say, "Come, let us go up to the mountain of the Lord, to the house of Jacob's God. There he will teach us his ways, and we will walk in his paths." For the Lord's teaching will go out from Zion; his word will go out from Jerusalem. The Lord will mediate between peoples and will settle disputes between strong nations far away. They will hammer their swords into plowshares and their spears into pruning hooks. Nation will no longer fight against nation, nor train for war anymore. Everyone will live in peace and prosperity, enjoying their own grapevines and fig trees, for there will be nothing to fear. The Lord of Heaven's Armies has made this promise!
>
> Micah 4:1–4; Cf. Isaiah 2:1–4

Micah reveals that during Jesus' millennial kingdom, people from "many nations" will stream to Jerusalem to have Jesus teach them how to walk in God's ways. Jesus will mediate between "strong nations"—that is, nations will experience conflict. However, as the Prince of Peace rules over the earth, "nation will no longer fight against nation."

The New Jerusalem

After the millennium, in the era of the "new heavens and new earth," nations will continue to be central to God's plan (Revelation 21:1, 23–26). Each nation's diversity will be celebrated when they "present their glory" (splendor) to God in the New Jerusalem (Revelation 21:1–2, 23–26). Examples of past splendor help us understand a bit of the future glory that will be presented to God in the New Jerusalem, including the architecture of ancient Greece, the Cedars of Lebanon, the cultural arts of France, the diamonds of Africa, and the inventions of China.

Among the concluding insights of the Bible, John affirms God's glorious continuous plan for nations stating: "On either side of the river was the tree of life … and the leaves of the tree were for the healing of the nations" (Revelation 22:2). Rather than becoming obsolete, nations will experience the health and wholeness God always intended.

As far as we can see into the future using the biblical lens, separate nations are part of God's unfolding plan.

Divine Destiny

God's dealings with nations throughout the Bible foreshadow God's numerous interactions with America. In 1778, George Washington wrote:

> The hand of Providence has been so conspicuous in all of this, that he must be worse than an infidel that lacks faith, and more than wicked, that has not gratitude enough to acknowledge His [God's] obligations [to us].[14]

America's history is replete with accounts of God intervening. Here is but a sampling concerning America's birth and protection.

The Battle of Monongahela

It is said that George Washington had nine lives, dodging bullets, serious illness, and all manner of perils. During the Battle of Monongahela of the French and Indian War, the colonists were suffering heavy losses when Washington entered the battle with a bad headache and a high fever. Though he had two horses shot out from under him, four bullets put through his coat, and his hat shot off his head, America's soon-to-be first president was protected to fight another day. [15]

The Battle of Long Island

And fight he did throughout the Revolutionary War. During the Battle of Long Island, which could have spelled defeat for the fledgling nation, Britain's powerful navy was on the brink of assaulting the Continental Army. To save lives, Washington wanted to evacuate his soldiers, but the odds were severely against him. Suddenly, a fog bank rolled in, allowing Washington and his men to escape to safety, protecting them for ultimate victory seven years later. [16]

Exposing Benedict Arnold

Several odd "coincidences" led to the discovery of Benedict's Arnold's treasonous plan to hand over West Point to the British. Due to the surprising capture of British Major John Andre, Arnold's co-conspirator, who was dressed as a civilian with the details of West Point hidden in his boot, the entire plot was exposed and thwarted. In a letter to one of his colonels, Washington wrote, "In no instance since the commencement of the War has the interposition of Providence appeared more conspicuous than in the rescue of ... West Point." On September 26, 1780, he wrote, "Treason of the blackest dye was yesterday discovered ... Happily, the treason has been timely discovered to prevent the fatal misfortune. The providential train of circumstances which led to it affords the most convincing proof that the Liberties of America are the object of divine protection."[17]

The War of 1812

During the War of 1812, God used the weather to rescue the young nation and an image of a now-dead Washington. Dolly Madison had saved a portrait of George Washington, which was on display in the White House. Under assault by the British, Madison saved the portrait while fleeing, just as the enemy attempted to set fire to the nation's capital. But God would not have it and whipped up a rain-laden tornado (one of seven in D.C.'s history) to quench the flames and terrify the British.[18]

Pearl Harbor

While the Japanese attack was meant to decimate America's navy, all but two ships were repaired, and key onshore resources like oil depots and repair shops were spared.[19]

The Battle of the Bulge

This infamous World War II battle in Belgium took 12,000 American lives, prompting Germany to demand that Brigadier General Anthony McAuliffe surrender. He is said to have replied, "NUTS!" to the ire and surprise of the German major. General George S. Patton, inspired by McAuliffe's snarky response, commissioned a prayer to be quickly written, printed, and distributed to 250,000 troops to lift harsh weather that was impeding Patton's rescue. The weather promptly cleared, and the army was saved.[20]

Presidential Protection

Many U.S. presidents miraculously survived multiple assassination attempts. Andrew Jackson, Theodore Roosevelt, George W. Bush, Bill Clinton, Ronald Reagan, Gerald Ford, and Donald Trump are among those whose lives were preserved. Who knows how many more rescues did not make the headlines.[21]

God cares about individual nations, including ours.

Our Response

From Genesis through the New Age, the creation and duration of individual nations matter to God. This is at odds with the current spirit of the age, a mindset that promotes globalism—a far-reaching governance that Satan and his dominion of darkness long to rule.

Even if the Bible teaches that just before Jesus' return globalists will succeed in ruling the world for a brief time, it is imperative that we understand what is taking place. Christians must not advocate or inadvertently aid and abet such a system. We are to stand against it, always representing God's purposes for individual sovereign nations. For those who pick up the forerunner mantle, we must alert others to God's purposes for nations, including God's purposes for America, while warning the body of Christ of globalism.

• • •

God's care for America and His protection has been evident numerous times. Yet, America is in a very different place than it was even a generation ago. This reality leads us to some hard questions. Is God removing His hand of blessing and protection? Is there a greater threat to America than the battle of the ages or giving up our national sovereignty to globalists? It is to the answers to these questions that we must turn to next.

OUR GREATEST THREAT

*For the Lord is a God who knows,
and by him deeds are weighed.*

1 Samuel 2:3 NIV

The affairs of nations take place before a God who knows and sees and hears (Proverbs 15:3). Biblical history proves that nations that behave the way America is behaving right now are not blessed by God. They are destroyed by God. America's greatest threat is not Satan, globalization, foreign invasion, cultural decay, or a political party. Our greatest threat is God Himself.

To suggest that God is our greatest threat might sound as if I am misrepresenting God's character or missing a Scriptural principle that pardons America's waywardness. However, the Bible describes God's righteous judgments from its first pages, where He sends a global flood, to its final pages, where Mystery Babylon is destroyed by God with fire. Even heads of state will look upon Babylon appalled at "the smoke rising from her charred remains" (Revelation 18:9, see verses 1-24).

Often overlooked, at Jesus' second coming, His first order of business will be to judge the nations. John tells us:

The armies of heaven, dressed in the finest of pure white linen, followed him [Jesus] on white horses. From his mouth came a sharp sword to strike down the nations. He will rule them with an iron rod. He will release the fierce wrath of God, the Almighty, like juice flowing from a winepress. On his robe at his thigh was written this title: King of all kings and Lord of all lords.

Revelation 19:14–16

Jesus, the very One who loves humanity, died for us, and forgives all who come to Him in faith, will "strike down the nations" and "release the fierce wrath of God." Contrary to popular belief, God's judgment of nations, even post-cross and post-Pentecost, is consistent with His character and how He holds people accountable for their actions.

Nations in the Balance

Events were escalating toward Judah's final national judgment in 586 B.C. Genuine prophets—stating what false prophets denied—leveled their laser beam jeremiads at Judah's stubborn defiance of God's will and ways. These warnings were followed by an urgent call for heart-searching repentance. However, mid-warning, God stopped to explain how He judges every nation on earth:

> At one moment I might speak concerning a nation or concerning a kingdom to uproot it, to tear it down, or to destroy *it*; if that nation against which I have spoken turns from its evil, I will relent of the disaster that I planned to bring on it. Or at *another* moment I might speak concerning a nation or concerning a kingdom to build up or to plant *it*; if it does evil in My sight by not obeying My voice, then I will relent of the good with which I said that I would bless it.
>
> Jeremiah 18:7–10 NASB

Jeremiah's dictation from God reveals this timeless principle: *God weighs every nation in the balance.* In other words, based on what the people choose, each nation will move toward God's favor and blessing or toward inciting God's judgment.

Age of Grace

Pondering Jeremiah's principle leaves us with a serious question: Does this God who punishes nations fit with living in the "age of grace," an age when sin has already been covered by Christ's death on the cross?

Some Old Covenant practices established by God—such as animal sacrifice—were replaced or discontinued because of the New Covenant. However, how God interacts with nations is not one of those practices. Put another way, Jesus' blood shed on the cross takes away the sin and eternal punishment of everyone who is born again by His Spirit, but does nothing to absolve the ongoing wickedness of nations. Why? Because rather than loving and following the living God, these nations are living in rebellion to Him.

Highlighted in the previous chapter, Paul affirms God's creation of nations and teaches that nations continue to be birthed or removed under His purview (Acts 17:26). This truth, coupled with Jeremiah's principle, reveal that the people who comprise a nation have significant say over how things turn out—and this includes America today.

Paul's teaching echoes a similar principle expressed by Job: "He [God] builds up nations, and he destroys them. He expands nations, and he abandons them" (Job 12:23). How then does God decide whether a nation will be built up or suffer ruin? Again, the outcome of each nation is based upon that nation's responsiveness to God's voice (Jeremiah 18:7–10).

Regarding God's abandonment of a nation—something that can also happen during the "age of grace"—pastor and author John MacArthur calls this divine distancing "the wrath of abandonment."[1] When God removes His hand of protection, a nation becomes vulnerable to foreign aggression or to destroying itself from within through hyperinflation, national debt, civil war, moral decay, and government corruption.

In contrast, if an individual, church, or nation draws near to God through humility, prayer, and repentance, God will draw near to them (James 4:8; 2 Chronicles 7:14; Lamentations 3:57). Connecting this truth to Job's observation, Jeremiah's principle, and Paul's affirmation, drawing God's presence is the right pursuit to see God spare a nation.

Not Only Israel

Many of the detailed accounts of God weighing a nation in the balance are centered on His chosen people, the nation of Israel. However, throughout Scripture, we see God treating Gentile nations the same.

In 539 BC, the Babylonian Empire came to a sudden end at the hands of innovative, respected, and celebrated Cyrus the Great, the first emperor of the Persian Empire. Babylon's walls were widely considered impregnable, but through divine orchestration, Cyrus' army devised a clever plan to divert the Euphrates River, which went through and around the city, to lower the water level. This gave Cyrus' army an opportune moment to dig under the city walls, invade, and defeat the Babylonians in a single night.[2]

At the exact time Cyrus was about to execute this surprise attack, God wrote a foreboding message on the palace wall to Belshazzar, the king of Babylon. This pronouncement was interpreted by God's servant Daniel:

Mene means 'numbered'—God has numbered the days of your reign and has brought it to an end.

Tekel means 'weighed'—you have been weighed on the balances and have not measured up.

Parsin means 'divided'—your kingdom has been divided and given to the Medes and Persians.

Daniel 5:26–28

Daniel states that God "weighed" the king, Belshazzar, the representative head of Babylon, "on the balances" and found him to be wicked. God then gave his kingdom over to the Medes and Persians. Here we see God interacting with a Gentile nation in the same way that He did with Israel. Paul's teaching and Daniel's revelation agree: God appoints the times of nations and brings them to an end. The implications for all nations, including America, are enormous.

God Blesses Nations

Nineveh, the capital city of the Assyrian Empire, is an example of God weighing a Gentile nation and finding it culpable of great evil. Then, after national repentance, God weighed Nineveh again and chose to bless it.

Under God's direction, the reluctant prophet Jonah declared, "Forty days from now Nineveh will be destroyed!" (Jonah 3:4). Given no hope of averting judgment, the Ninevites still chose to humble themselves by fasting—no food or water allowed—not even for the animals. Remarkably, the king humbled himself by replacing his regal attire with burlap and laid in ashes—outward signs of his inward sorrow over his nation's sin. He also called everyone to fervently pray to God, turn from sin, and cease all acts of violence (Jonah 3:5–9).

Jonah writes, "When God saw what they had done and how they had put a stop to their evil ways, he changed his mind and did not carry out the destruction he had threatened" (Jonah 3:10). Humbling themselves and repenting, the Ninevites averted destruction.

God weighed Babylon and Nineveh—one was replaced by an emerging empire; the other was mercifully spared. When God executes judgment or extends mercy, it is always connected to the behavior of the people—behavior that is either rooted in pride and wickedness, or in humility and obedience to the one true God.

God treats Gentile nations no differently than ancient Israel; nor nations in Scripture differently than nations today. Old Testament or New, then and now, if a nation can be blessed by God, a nation can be judged by God. Former traveling revivalist Laine Johnson challenged congregations with this powerful truth: "God is America's greatest threat. But He is also our greatest hope."

Corrective Shakings

Like any good parent, God employs disciplinary measures—often increasingly forceful—as means to correct a nation. His goal is to redirect destructive mindsets and behaviors to ones that glorify Him and are beneficial to all.

The prophet Amos shares numerous examples of God sending corrective shakings to Israel, including famines, droughts, disease, plagues, and foreign aggression (Amos 4:6–11). The people refused to turn back to God, so God promised final judgment with this terrifying declaration: "Prepare to meet your God ... you people of Israel!" (Amos 4:12).

I believe evidence abounds that America has also experienced corrective shakings that, left unheeded, will also result in final judgment. America's recent shakings include 9-11, Hurricane Katrina, the 2008–'09 economic meltdown, the 2020 race riots, increasing political animosity, the COVID pandemic, and the devastating Maui fires in 2023.

Spiritual Light and Opportunity

In his book *Is God on America's Side*, Erwin Lutzer asserts that God judges nations based on how much spiritual light and opportunity they are given (Luke 12:47–48). He defines light as biblical teaching, truth, revelation of God, knowledge, and the related blessings thereof.[3] The spiritual light America has received outshines every nation except for ancient Israel:

- Many of America's Founding Fathers adhered to biblical principles and morality.
- America's first colleges were established to impart a Christian worldview and to train young men for the ministry.
- Bible verses adorn buildings and monuments throughout America's capital.
- Highlighting powerful moves of God where multitudes came to faith, America is known as the nation of the Great Awakenings.
- Until the 1961 Supreme Court ruling removing prayer from schools, many of our public institutions such as courthouses and schools displayed the Ten Commandments, nativity scenes, and Bible verses.

- God blessed America as "The land of opportunity."
- Americans have always had access to the Bible, and today, every translation is accessible online.
- Americans can learn about and worship God continuously through church gatherings, Christian radio, music, online messages, podcasts, Christian books, and conferences.
- America is known as the nation "with a church on every corner."

If judgment is based on how much spiritual light and opportunity a nation has received, where does this leave America? Itinerant preacher and author Leonard Ravenhill (1907–1994) raises the inconvenient question, if God destroyed the Sodomites who had no Bible—nor any of the other benefits listed above—would He not be just in destroying America?[4]

Our Response

The author of Hebrews warns:

> Dear friends, if we deliberately continue sinning after we have received knowledge of the truth, there is no longer any sacrifice that will cover these sins. There is only the terrible expectation of God's judgment and the raging fire that will consume his enemies. For anyone who refused to obey the law of Moses was put to death without mercy on the testimony of two or three witnesses. Just think how much worse the punishment will be for those who have trampled on the Son of God, and have treated the blood of the covenant, which made us holy, as if it were common and unholy, and have insulted and disdained the Holy Spirit who brings God's mercy to us.

Hebrews 10:26–29

We would do well to ponder this passage, both as individuals and as a nation.

. . .

In addition to God weighing nations based on how much spiritual light and opportunity they are given, how else is God assessing America? It is to this topic that we must turn to next.

AMERICA IN THE BALANCE

Hear this, you priests! Pay attention, house of Israel! Listen, you of the house of the king! For the judgment applies to you.

Hosea 5:1 NASB

Ten years after 9-11, a friend and I got away to seek the Lord on behalf of America. We were troubled by our nation's immorality, corrupt leadership, and a silent church. Going into this prayer retreat, neither of us expected something dramatic to happen. God had other plans.

Near the end of the first day, without warning I sensed God's presence in the room in a remarkable way. It was the *kabod* of God—the weightiness of God's glory—that had come upon me. In the next few moments, God impressed upon me that America was culpable of great wickedness and would experience a great humbling—a devastating judgment that would be far more consequential than 9-11.

This experience had a profound effect on me and further convinced me that America is in danger. Yet, I wondered, apart from such subjective experiences, how can someone know a nation's status before God?

A New Paradigm

In other words, if Jeremiah's principle teaches that God weighs each nation in the balance, how can we discern which way the scale is tipping and how far? The answer to this question came over time as I grasped a biblical paradigm that objectively reveals the status of a nation before God.

I call this assessment tool the Church-Society-Government Paradigm, which is based on answering three questions:
- What is the church saying and doing (or not saying and doing)?
- What does society want?
- Where is the government—federal, state, and local—leading us?

When these three spheres—the church, society, and government—seek to honor God, that nation experiences God's blessing. As Jeremiah relayed, they are planted, built up, and thrive. When these three spheres converge in rebellion to God, that nation will experience corrective shakings and, if left unheeded, terrifying final judgment.

Almost everything taking place in culture and reported in the news is addressed in the Bible. Therefore, we can objectively discern America's status before God. Before assessing America's status, let's look at how this paradigm is presented in Scripture.

A Biblical Approach

The Bible addresses the Church-Society-Government Paradigm over thirty-five times.[1] In other passages, God singles out one or two of these spheres. At the time Jeremiah was commissioned to start his public ministry, God commanded him to contend against all three spheres:

Get up and prepare for action. Go out and tell them everything I tell you to say. Do not be afraid of them, or I will make you look foolish in front of them. For see, today I have made you strong like a fortified city that cannot be captured, like an iron pillar or a bronze wall. You will stand against the whole land—the kings, officials, priests, and people of Judah. They will fight you, but they will fail. For I am with you, and I will take care of you. I, the Lord, have spoken!"

Jeremiah 1:17–19

The "priests" were the ancient equivalent of today's church leadership. The "people of Judah" were the ancient equivalent of modern society. The "kings" and "officials" were the ancient equivalent of America's government sphere. Jeremiah was tasked to "stand against the whole land"—an intimidating mission of taking on all three spheres at once! This is why God urged him to hold on to His promises.

Shortly after his calling, God addressed these three spheres during Jeremiah's initial prophetic message to the nation:

Listen to the word of the Lord, people of Jacob—all you families of Israel! This is what the Lord says: "What did your ancestors find wrong with me that led them to stray so far from me?" … The priests did not ask, 'Where is the Lord?' Those who taught my word ignored me, the rulers turned against me."

Jeremiah 2:4–5, 8

Society, addressed as "people of Jacob," "all you families of Israel," and "ancestors," was reprimanded for departing from the one true God. The priests, equivalent to today's church leadership, should have asked why God was no longer active throughout the nation, but did not. And "the rulers," the government realm, had rejected God.

Continuing this scathing address, God addresses the church, society, and government spheres again:

> Israel is like a thief who feels shame only when he gets caught. They, their kings and officials, priests, and prophets—all are alike in this.
>
> Jeremiah 2:26

Later, when the Babylonians held Jerusalem under siege, the priests, society, and rulers chose to obey God by freeing their fellow Jews from enslavement. However, as soon as God removed Judah's immediate threat—the Babylonians left to fight another enemy—all three spheres enslaved the people again (Jeremiah 34:1–22). Instead of heartfelt repentance, the nation chose to do what was expedient. In response, God declared final judgment on the entire nation:

> Because you have broken the terms of our covenant, I will cut you apart just as you cut apart the calf when you walked between its halves to solemnize your vows. Yes, I will cut you apart, whether you are officials of Judah or Jerusalem [government], court officials [government], priests [church], or common people [society]—for you have broken your oath. I will give you to your enemies, and they will kill you. Your bodies will be food for the vultures and wild animals.
>
> Jeremiah 34:18–20

Eleven years later, Judah experienced God's final judgment, a crushing defeat at the hands of the Babylonians. Jeremiah not only records the widespread loss of life but also the physical ruins of the capital city: The palace (the seat of government), the homes of the people (society), and the temple (the ancient equivalent of a church building) were burned to the ground (Jeremiah 52:12–13). It is as if, through these smoldering buildings, God put an exclamation point on what was weighed on His scale and found lacking.

Reset

Sometimes, God protects a remnant of true believers within the church, society, and government spheres to reset a nation. During Ahab's reign over Israel, the prophet Elijah felt so overwhelmed by cultural evil that he cried out for God to take his life. God answered Elijah's cry, not by taking his life, but by sharing His plan to replace evil kings with righteous kings (government), replace Elijah's ministry with Elisha's ministry (church leadership), and replace the sway of wicked people with the sway of seven thousand who had not bent their knees to Baal (society) (1 Kings 19:1–21).

Meanwhile, in Judah, King Ahaziah's power-hungry mother, Athaliah, killed her grandsons to secure her position on the throne. Yet, one of Ahaziah's sons, Joash, was hidden by Jehoida, the chief priest. Six years later, Athaliah was killed and replaced by the rightful king, Joash. The church, society, and government spheres converged, and Judah experienced God's blessing:

> Then Jehoiada [church leadership] made a covenant between the Lord and the king [government] and the people [society] that they would be the Lord's people... And all the people of the land [society] went over to the temple of Baal and tore it down ... Jehoiada the priest [church leadership] stationed guards at the Temple of the Lord. Then the commanders [government], the Carite mercenaries, the palace guards [government], and all the people of the land [society] escorted the king [government] from the Temple of the

Lord.... And the king took his seat on the royal throne. So all the people of the land rejoiced.

2 Kings 11:17–20 (emphasis added)

God made a way for the righteous remnant within the church, society, and government spheres to influence the entire nation, even to renew the covenant with Him. When these three demographics converge for good, God will change a nation, and there will be quite a celebration!

In each of these examples, the church, society, and government either converge to honor God and experience blessing or unify to reject God and experience devastation. These are the areas we must vigilantly give our attention to today—the three spheres that God weighs in the balance.

The Paradigm in History

In 1776, historian and British Parliament member Edward Gibbon published *The History of the Decline and Fall of the Roman Empire*. Near the end of Gibbon's book, he lists the reasons for the collapse of the Roman Empire, which had held the civilized world together for more than 500 years. Many of his conclusions reveal at least one aspect of the Church-Society-Government Paradigm. In part, Rome fell because of:

- Excessive spending by Rome's central government.
  - The government was leading the empire into bankruptcy.
  - National debt is an indicator that God is rejecting a nation (Deuteronomy 28:12, 44).
- Overindulgence in luxury.

- Society craved money, comfort, and ease.
- Indulgence and greed reveals society is at odds with God's purposes (Amos 6:1–7; James 5:4–6; Revelation 18:1–24).
- Widespread sexual immorality and easy divorce destroyed the integrity of the family.
  - The nuclear family, the foundational building block of society, was undermined.
  - God hates sexual sin, immorality, and divorce (Matthew 15:19; 1 Corinthians 10:7–8; 2 Peter 2:6–7; Malachi 2:26).
- The spread of effeminacy—men looking and acting like girls.
  - Society and the government accepted gender fluidity.
  - God created males and females and is repulsed by gender fluidity (Deuteronomy 22:5; 1 Corinthians 6:9–10).
- Disregard for religion.
  - Although the early church made significant inroads into Roman culture, eventually, her teachings were broadly rejected.
  - God will pour out His righteous anger on those who reject Him (Romans 1:18–2:11).

Gibbon's conclusions were applied to the United States in 1968 when Las Colinas city developer Ben Carpenter warned a convention of businessmen about America's dangerous trajectory in his speech, "Leaving the Problem to Others."[2] Using Gibbon's summary, Carpenter challenged his colleagues to wake-up and address these issues emerging throughout culture.

Concerned over 50 years ago, Carpenter likely had little idea that America's government would eventually find itself awash in tens of trillions of dollars of debt. Carpenter would have had only a glimpse of what we see today with surging LGBTQ lifestyles, including government officials debating whether biological boys and girls are, in fact, male or female. He would have had little idea of the degree to which society would increasingly pursue money, comfort, luxury, and entertainment. At the time, he would have had little idea of the ubiquitous nature of "easy divorce" that would soon be embraced one state at a time through the passing of no-fault divorce laws. He would have had no idea that marriage would be redefined to include the gay community. He would have only partially witnessed the erosion of Christian values and the worldliness of the church that we see today.

Nonetheless, a generation ago, Carpenter filled the forerunner role by discerning what was happening, anticipating what was likely coming, and warning others. Scholars have also drawn parallels between the immorality of ancient Rome and America, but Carpenter models how any Christian can give voice to what is taking place.

America in the Balance

What the church is saying and doing, what society wants, and the direction set by the government are God's measurements to decide the future of a nation. Let's ask the three assessment questions in relation to open borders, abortion, LGBTQ lifestyles, and our nation maintaining a Christian worldview.

Open Borders

An open border with Mexico, allowing undocumented illegal immigrants to enter the U.S., has been a contentious issue for years.

As noted as part of his vision for a New World Order, President Bush longed for open borders over thirty years ago.

Dr. Stephen Turley, an internationally recognized scholar, TurleyTalks blogger, and Greek and Theology professor, connects illegal immigration to globalism: "As long as there is globalization, there will be globalists, those who believe that national borders are constituents of larger "unjust" social boundaries."[3] We know what God thinks about globalism (see Chapter Three), and thus, what God thinks of open borders being a globalist strategy to bring about a New World Order. With this in mind, let's look at what the assessment questions reveal:

- Where is the government leading us?
  - In 2022, the number of illegal immigrants crossing the U.S. border topped out at 2.76 million, a million more than the previous record high.[4]
  - In 2023, unprecedented numbers, verified by the federal government, showed higher than ever illegal immigration at the U.S border, with "1.7 million known gotaways" since 2021, while the government was "incentivizing and facilitating the entry of otherwise inadmissible aliens into the United States at a scale never before seen."[5]
- What does society want?
  - Twenty years of polling consistently shows that about 60% of Americans are somewhat or very concerned about illegal immigrants coming over U.S. borders. The remaining 40% hold no opinion or are in favor of open borders.[6]
- What is the church saying and doing?
  - Although God explains His view on open borders, nations, and globalism, the church remains silent.

Conclusion: Though a majority of U.S. citizens want to maintain border security, the church and government spheres have failed to understand the biblical position. America is weighed by God and found wanting.

Abortion

The Bible teaches that all people are created in the image of God, including the yet-to-be-born, and God hates the shedding of innocent blood. In 2022, the U.S. Supreme Court overturned *Roe v. Wade*, stating that the U.S. Constitution does not speak to abortion and left the issue for each state to decide. With this in mind, let's see what the three assessment questions reveal:

- Where is the government leading us?
  - Since the Supreme Court's landmark decision in 2022, most state governments have either passed laws to protect the yet-to-be-born or passed laws to expand abortion rights.[7]
- What does society want?
  - As of 2024, Americans are split. Twenty-two states protect the life of the unborn, 22 states allow late-term abortions, and six states and the District of Columbia protect life in some circumstances.[8]
- What is the church saying and doing?
  - With the exception of recognizing pro-life issues on January 22 each year on the anniversary of the Supreme Court's decision to legalize abortion in 1973, the church generally says and does nothing.

Conclusion: Until July 2022, all 50 states and the District of Columbia provided abortion services. Currently, our nation is divided. However, with abortion still legal in 22 states and to a lesser degree in seven more states and the District of Columbia, the nation's daily abortion count continues to climb. The church, prone to stay silent on controversial issues, needs to find its voice and provide practical ways for Christians to contend for life in their communities, as well as at the state and local levels of government. The shedding of innocent blood is a primary reason God will judge America.[9] America is being weighed by God and is found wanting.

LGBTQ Lifestyles
What about LGBTQ lifestyles, all of which are contrary to God's design?

- Where is the government leading us?
  - U.S. Congress passed The Respect for Marriage Act in 2022, which the President enthusiastically signed into law. This legislation protects gay marriage, transgender lifestyles, and any other arrangement one desires, regardless of future Supreme Court rulings. At the signing ceremony, Senate Majority Leader Chuck Schumer stated, "By enacting this law, we are sending a message to LGBTQ Americans everywhere. You, too, deserve dignity. You, too, deserve equality. That is about as an American ideal as they come." Schumer went on to warmly declare that the day his daughter was married to "a beautiful young lady" was one of the happiest days of his life.[10]
  - President Biden stated, "Today I sign into law The Respect for Marriage Act...Today, we celebrate our progress from

Hawaii, the first state to declare that to deny same-sex marriage is unconstitutional, to Massachusetts; the first state to recognize marriage equality…There is nothing more decent, more dignified, and more American than what we are about to do here today."[11]

- What does society want?
    - From 2012 to 2022, the number of Americans who practice LGBTQ lifestyles doubled from 3.5% to 7.2%. The youngest adult demographic surveyed in 2022, 18–24 years old, showed that 20% identify with one or more LGBTQ lifestyles.[12]
    - In 2021, for the first time, 70% of Americans were in favor of gay marriage, with 84% of adults 18–34 approving, and for the first time, 60% of adults fifty-five and over approving.[13]
- What is the church saying and doing?
    - Although human sexuality is, first and foremost, a biblical issue, one that weighs on God's heart deeply, the church is typically silent.

Conclusion: The church, society, and government have been weighed by God, and America is found wanting.

Maintaining a Biblical Worldview

- Where is the government leading us?
    - Because of the separation of church and state, the government removed prayer and the centrality of the Bible from public schools in 1961. Since 1980, the government

has systematically removed the Ten Commandments from public buildings.
- What does society want?
  - People have been deceived to believe that the Bible is bigoted, narrow-minded, full of hate, or irrelevant, resulting in 96% of Americans no longer holding to a biblical worldview.[14]
- What is the church saying and doing?
  - Although discipling believers to hold a biblical worldview is one of the primary purposes of the church, only 13% of those who professed to be born-again Christians in 2023 held a biblical worldview. Apparently, while many churches energetically speak on an array of topics and often provide lively worship, 87% of those who call themselves Christians do not understand what the Bible teaches about sin, Jesus, and salvation.[15]

Conclusion: The church, society, and government are not honoring God's Word; therefore, God will not honor us. America has been weighed and found wanting.

Would America fare any better if we put our low regard for marriage through the questions of the Church-Society-Government assessment tool? Would the conclusion regarding the legalization of recreational marijuana come out any differently? Would the emerging acceptance of pedophilia, now referred to with the more palatable term "minor attraction," be assessed with a different outcome? Would running pornography through the Church-Society-Government Paradigm reveal a more favorable outcome for America?

Reflecting on this assessment, would God be unfair to send greater corrective judgments or final judgment to America? How close are we to having Daniel's "writing on the wall" becoming America's reality (Daniel 5:5–6, 25–28)?

Our Response

With the biblical lens of God weighing nations in the balance, corrective shakings, final judgment, and the Church-Society-Government Paradigm in place, it is imperative that every Christian assess America's status before God. Once we have made this assessment, we must cry out to God for mercy, warn others of our nation's dangerous trajectory, and call people to wholeheartedly turn back to God. This is what biblical forerunners did. So must we.

• • •

Is it possible that America's situation is far worse than what we have looked at so far? It is to this topic that we must turn to next.

HAVE WE CROSSED A LINE?

Even if Moses and Samuel stood before me pleading for these people, I wouldn't help them. Away with them! Get them out of my sight!

Jeremiah 15:1

Called by God, David Wilkerson (1931–2011) left his rural Pennsylvania church in 1958 to lead gang members in New York City to faith in Jesus. Wilkerson shares extraordinary accounts of lost young people experiencing radically changed lives in his bestseller *The Cross and the Switchblade*. Seeing the needs of those he ministered led him to launch Teen Challenge, a faith-based substance abuse rehabilitation program.[1] Today Teen Challenge has grown to more than 1,400 locations in 129 countries,[2] still seeing remarkable results.[3]

Wilkerson also started Time Square Church in 1987, reaching the homeless, criminals, and drug addicts wandering the streets of Manhattan. Wilkerson, working alongside other churches and ministries, saw safe clean streets become the norm. Prayers for the city were also answered in the government sphere with better public policy helping to improve conditions.

Unexpected Warning

If anyone should have proclaimed that God was about to save America through a sweeping spiritual awakening, it should have been Wilkerson. If gang lords, murderers, prostitutes, thieves, and drug addicts were undeniably changed by the gospel and large portions of New York City were transformed, why not all of America?

Though many observed at this time that God was doing a wonderful work in numerous locations throughout our nation and predicted that God was about to save America, Wilkerson authored two books in the 1970s warning of impending danger: *The Vision* and *Racing Toward Judgment*. In 1998, Wilkerson published *America's Last Call*, again alerting our nation to its dangerous trajectory before a holy God. Wilkerson states:

> Our nation right now is receiving its final call to repentance...I say this not because I've had a dream or vision about it. Rather, I have simply studied God's Word—and I [have] discerned from the Scriptures that God is dealing with America in the same way that He's dealt with all nations who have forsaken Him.[4]

Similar to God's command to Jeremiah to cease praying for his nation,[5] Wilkerson continues:

> Do you see what God is saying here? God is saying, "The nation has crossed a line—and I won't hear any prayers on their behalf!" Beloved, a time comes when people sin so persistently, grieving God so deeply, that a line is crossed. God determines to bring judgment—and no amount of prayer can change it.
>
> This happens time after time in Scripture—and it's happening to America right now! God says, "I've had enough of your bloodshed,

your idolatry, you're pushing me out [of your lives]. Go ahead, make your intercession and pleas—but I won't hear any of it!"⁶

Wilkerson believed that America had crossed the line of no return and that God would bring devastating judgment. This is why he continued—even while seeing extraordinary fruit—to fervently warn everyone he could of what was coming. His message and tone are remarkably similar to what God shared with me in 2011. (See my opening remarks in the previous chapter.)

When God Contends

Like Wilkerson, I believe the judgment that is coming to America will be severe. A shift from God blessing a nation to God contending against a nation does not happen quickly. Yet, according to Scripture, it does happen—and more frequently than we might think.

Through the prophet Hosea, God declared His deep-abiding love for His chosen people:

> I have been the Lord your God ever since I brought you out of Egypt... I took care of you in the wilderness, in that dry and thirsty land.
>
> Hosea 13:4–5

God affirms His love for Israel by comparing Himself to a faithful husband married to a harlot. Even though Israel was prostituting herself, God went to great lengths to tenderly draw Israel back to once again be a faithful wife to Him. God even describes Himself as a loving parent who taught the Israelites to walk, led them by the hand, cared for them, guided them with "bonds of love," lifted burdens off them, and kneeled down from heaven to feed them (Hosea 11:3–4). However, God also explains why He became estranged from His own people:

> But when you had eaten and were satisfied, you became proud and forgot me.
>
> Hosea 13:6

Comfort, pride, and a short memory caused the Israelites to drift from God.[7] God continued to pursue them, but the people played the harlot by worshiping pagan gods (Hosea 3:1; 4:11–14; 9:1; 13:1–2). They rejected knowledge in general, and God's Word specifically, with their religious leaders as spiritually lost as the people (Hosea 4:6–9). These realities became fertile soil for further wickedness to proliferate everywhere: stealing, adultery, murder, and all types of iniquity.[8]

Rather than God, the Israelites relied on other nations to defend them (Hosea 7:11; 8:8–9; 9:3;12:1). In the end, God warned Israel that they had "planted the wind" of sin and cultural chaos, but were about to "harvest the whirlwind" of devastating judgment (Hosea 8:7).

Because of Israel's hardened depravity and lawlessness, God described what was about to happen:

> So now I [God] will attack you like a lion, like a leopard that lurks along the road. Like a bear whose cubs have been taken away, I will tear out your heart. I will devour you like a hungry lioness and mangle you like a wild animal. You are about to be destroyed, O Israel—yes, by me, your only helper.
>
> Hosea 13:7–9

Not pretty. God is serious about rebellion; and if a nation persists, He will take decisive action.[9] This presents another timeless principle: *If God will fight against His own chosen people, He may choose to fight against any rebellious nation.* How then can a nation know whether it has crossed the line—a line where God has become her enemy?

Crossing the Line

God is patient, slow to anger, and abounds in love, but His patience with persistent systemic evil will run out. In this scenario, God grows weary of restraining His justice by giving people numerous chances to repent, only to be rejected again and again (Jeremiah 6:10–11; 15:6). Graciously, God provides the faithful remnant indicators when a nation has crossed the line and will face final judgment.

Prayer Denied

God is the God of answered prayer, but He also hides Himself from the wicked. God, personifying wisdom, explains:

> I called you so often, but you wouldn't come. I reached out to you, but you paid no attention. You ignored my advice and rejected the correction I offered. So I will laugh when you are in trouble! I will mock you when disaster overtakes you—when calamity overtakes you like a storm, when disaster engulfs you like a cyclone, and anguish and distress overwhelm you. When they cry for help, I will not answer. Though they anxiously search for me, they will not find me. For they hated knowledge and chose not to fear the Lord.
>
> Proverbs 1:24–29

Similarly, after identifying Judah's many sins, God was appalled that His people still expected Him to answer their prayers for national blessing. God said to Jeremiah, "Pray no more for these people, Jeremiah. Do not weep or pray for them, and don't beg me to help them, for I will not listen to you" (Jeremiah 7:16). Further God declared, "Even if Moses and Samuel stood before me pleading for these people, I wouldn't help them. Away with them! Get them out of my sight!" (Jeremiah 15:1).

As for those who maintained some version of religiosity, God said, "When they fast, I will pay no attention. When they present their burnt offerings and grain offerings to me, I will not accept them. Instead, I will devour them with war, famine, and disease" (Jeremiah 14:12). Israel's southern kingdom had crossed the line—a line in which final judgment awaited.

A hundred and fifty years prior, God responded to Amos's cries for Israel by stopping two judgments in real-time: locusts and fire. However, because the people refused to respond in humility and repentance, God sent another judgment—a final judgment—of which Amos was not allowed to plead with God. God had decided, "I will spare them no longer" (Amos 7:1–9).

Speaking through Isaiah, God said, "When you lift up your hands in prayer, I will not look. Though you offer many prayers, I will not listen, for your hands are covered with the blood of innocent victims" (Isaiah 1:15).

Today, too often, we believe God is obligated to answer our prayers for America's blessing. Even though our nation practices outright rebellion, we still expect God to jump at our requests. However, once God chooses not to hear the prayers of the people, including the righteous remnant, there is conclusive evidence that a nation has crossed the line and devastating judgment is coming.

Handed Over

God will hand people and nations over to pursue the full extent of their evil desires. Such a pursuit provokes the full extent of God's fury, that is God's wrath.

According to Paul, the first step to being handed over is to suppress the truth by denying God's existence. Next, hearts are darkened through foolish speculations, and people worship created things rather than the Creator. Then God turns them over to the lusts of their hearts, including same-sex attraction. When people no longer acknowledge the one true God, He hands them over to a moral freefall to "do things that should never be done" (Romans 1:18–28).

Paul continues:

Their lives became full of every kind of wickedness, sin, greed, hate, envy, murder, quarreling, deception, malicious behavior, and gossip. They are backstabbers, haters of God, insolent, proud, and boastful. They invent new ways of sinning, and they disobey their parents. They refuse to understand, break their promises, are heartless, and have no mercy. They know God's justice requires that those who do these things deserve to die, yet they do them anyway. Worse yet, they encourage others to do them, too.

Romans 1:29–32

No one is beyond the reach of the cross, yet Paul explains that those who continue to harden themselves against God will reach a point of no return. A point, which we are about to see, nations can also reach.

Paul reveals why God destroyed Sodom and Gomorrah. Society was so far gone that the men refused sexual relations with Lot's daughters, instead desiring to rape Lot's visitors—two angelic men. At some point prior to this lurid scene, God handed these people over to their own lusts. The next day, God destroyed these cities and the surrounding towns and villages (Genesis 19:1–29).

Jeremiah explains God's decision to hand over Israel's southern kingdom to its own passions. Notice the parallels of Jeremiah and

Paul's warnings regarding callousness, wickedness, rejecting God, greed, dishonesty, and shameless attitudes:

> [Jeremiah speaking:] To whom can I give warning? Who will listen when I speak? Their ears are closed, and they cannot hear. They scorn the word of the Lord. They don't want to listen at all. So now I am filled with the Lord's fury. Yes, I am tired of holding it in! [God speaking:] "I will pour out my fury on children playing in the streets and on gatherings of young men, on husbands and wives and on those who are old and gray. Their homes will be turned over to their enemies, as will their fields and their wives. For I will raise my powerful fist against the people of this land," says the Lord. "From the least to the greatest, their lives are ruled by greed. From prophets to priests, they are all frauds. They offer superficial treatments for my people's mortal wound. They give assurances of peace when there is no peace. Are they ashamed of their disgusting actions? Not at all—they don't even know how to blush! Therefore, they will lie among the slaughtered. They will be brought down when I punish them," says the Lord.
>
> Jeremiah 6:10–15

Before God's fury is poured out, God hands people and nations over to their own wicked desires. This, too, is evidence that a nation has crossed God's line and is facing final judgment.

Confusion Sets In

When a nation has reached a point of no return, the people fall into a spiritual stupor and moral drunkenness. God commanded Jeremiah:

> So tell them, "This is what the Lord, the God of Israel, says: May all your jars be filled with wine." And they will reply, "Of course! Jars are made to be filled with wine!" Then tell them, "No, this is what the Lord means: I will fill everyone in this land with drunkenness—

from the king sitting on David's throne to the priests and the prophets, right down to the common people of Jerusalem. I will smash them against each other, even parents against children," says the Lord. "I will not let my pity or mercy or compassion keep me from destroying them."

Jeremiah 13:12–14

Already drunk on wickedness, pride, and immorality, the government, religious leaders, and society are about to experience the devastation that comes when God sends cultural confusion and chaos.

When His line has been crossed, God will impair the decision-makers' thinking, which in turn brings greater confusion to the already wayward people. This time addressing Egypt, Isaiah records:

> The officials of Zoan are fools, and the officials of Memphis are deluded. The leaders of the people have led Egypt astray. The Lord has sent a spirit of foolishness on them, so all their suggestions are wrong. They cause Egypt to stagger like a drunk in his vomit. There is nothing Egypt can do.

Isaiah 19:13–15

Job explains: "He [God] deprives the leaders of the earth of their reason … They grope in darkness with no light; *he makes them stagger like drunkards*" (Job 12:24–25 NIV, emphasis added).

In the latter days, the same will happen to people who immerse themselves in luxury and sexual permissiveness: "For all the nations have drunk of the wine of the passion of her [Mystery Babylon's] immorality, and the kings of the earth have committed acts of immorality with her, and the merchants of the earth have become rich by the wealth of her sensuality" (Revelation 18:3 NASB). This season of drunkenness on immorality, worldliness, and pleasures is the last step before God brings final judgment.

As delusion and confusion overcome a nation, only those serious about God and living righteously will be saved. Prophesying before Israel's final judgment, Amos urged everyone to repent while there was still time:

> Do what is good and run from evil so that you may live! Then the Lord God of heaven's Armies will be your helper, just as you have claimed. Hate evil and love what is good; turn your courts into true halls of justice. Perhaps even yet the Lord God of Heaven's Armies will have mercy on the remnant of his people.

Amos 5:14–15

Israel is about to face final judgment, which will include an unspeakable death toll. But Amos reveals that a remnant can still be saved—and anyone can join that remnant through faith and repentance.

We see this same urgency when God calls the remnant out of the Babylonian system:

> Come away from her, my people. Do not take part in her sins, or you will be punished with her. For her sins are piled as high as heaven, and God remembers her evil deeds.

Revelation 18:4–5

Cultural confusion over right and wrong, coupled with a final call to repent, is another indicator that a nation is about to experience final judgment.

God Becomes the Enemy

When God identifies Himself as the enemy, a nation is in serious trouble. But is this even possible? Ezekiel explains:

After God had told the Israelites that they had replaced Him with useless idols, defied His will and ways, and had sinned worse than other nations, God said, "I myself, the Sovereign Lord, am now your enemy... I will punish you like I have never punished anyone before or ever will again."

Ezekiel 5:8–9

God showed His mercy and intervention on so many occasions that He expected Israel not to forsake Him again (Isaiah 63:7–9). However, Isaiah tells us that over a long period of time, "They [Israel] rebelled against him [God] and grieved his Holy Spirit. *So he became their enemy and fought against them*" (Isaiah 63:10, emphasis added). Isaiah records God speaking to a culture still celebrating their relationship with God, but utterly lost:

What sorrow awaits Ariel, the City of David. Year after year you celebrate your feasts. Yet I will bring disaster upon you, and there will be much weeping and sorrow. For Jerusalem will become what her name Ariel means—an altar covered with blood. *I will be your enemy*, surrounding Jerusalem and attacking its walls. I will build siege towers and destroy it.

Isaiah 29:1–3 (emphasis added)

The Assyrian army destroyed Israel in 721 B.C., and the Babylonians brought destruction to Judah in 586 B.C. Were these mere military conquests? Absolutely not. God revealed that He was behind it all. He was Israel's greatest threat, and that threat was fully realized when God declared that He had become their enemy.

His Ways

These passages reveal God's position on wickedness, His righteousness, and His willingness to act. God has revealed His ways to us.

Through understanding God's ways in the past, we can anticipate what God will do in the future. He never contradicts His written Word, which reveals His nature and character. Therefore, understanding who He is and His ways, as well as what is unfolding before our very eyes, is central to discovering God's message to us today.

We must ask if God has quit responding to our prayers to save our nation. Has He handed us over to a moral freefall? Are we experiencing the final cultural confusion before final judgment arrives? Has God positioned Himself as America's enemy?

Has America Crossed the Line?

Like Wilkerson, I too believe America has crossed the line and that we will likely face a devastating judgment. Let's look at a few additional reasons why this appears to be the case.

Proliferating Paganism

In his bestseller *The Return of the Gods,* Jonathan Cahn asserts that America's departure from the one true God has created the conditions for ancient pagan gods, and the evil spirits that are behind them, to enter America.[10] Jesus supports this assertion:

> When an evil spirit leaves a person, it goes into the desert, seeking rest but finding none. Then it says, "I will return to the person I came from." So it returns and finds its former home empty, swept, and in order. Then the spirit finds seven other spirits more evil than itself, and they all enter the person and live there. And so that person is worse off than before. *That will be the experience of this evil generation.*
>
> Matthew 12:43–45 (emphasis added)

Noting Jesus' last phrase, Cahn explains that Jesus' teaching applies to a "generation, a culture, a civilization." There is no neutral ground. If a nation once knew the presence and power of God and rejects Him, it will be filled with evil spirits and become worse than before.[11] Cahn summarizes that a pre-Christian generation might experience an evil dictator, such as those who ruled the Roman Empire, but "a post-Christian civilization will produce a Hitler or Stalin."[12]

Cahn believes that, like ancient Israel, America is now replacing God with other gods and the wicked spirits that accompany them. These gods are not typically worshiped in temples, and Americans are rarely aware that they are following them. Nevertheless, the pagan practices of these gods have taken hold throughout society. These gods have taken on new identities fitting to the 21st century and have chosen to:

> Come upon the movers and influencers of modern culture and make them their instruments ... They inhabit our institutions, walk the halls of governments, cast votes in our legislatures, guide our corporations, gaze out of our skyscrapers, perform on our stages, and teach in our universities ... They instruct our children and initiate them into their ways. They incite the multitudes. They drive otherwise rational people into irrationality and some to frenzies, just as they had done in ancient times. They demand worship, our veneration, our submission, our sacrifices ... The gods are here.[13]

Baal, the chief god of the Canaanite pantheon, sought to separate the nation of Israel from the one true God and then replace Him altogether.[14] Just as this false deity deceived the Israelites to remove the Ten Commandments, the spirits behind Baal used the U.S. Supreme Court in 1980 to remove the Ten Commandments from public schools, then government buildings, then all of America.[15] In the 1960s, prayer was removed from public schools, and then the Bible was no longer allowed to be used as a primary text, nor a devotional source, something that had endured as part of our nation's education from the early days of colonial America.[16] This separated the coming generations of students from the God that had birthed and blessed America beyond measure. Tragically, these legal rulings gave the gods new freedoms to roam throughout the land of the free and the home of the brave. Cahn summarizes:

> Since the Word and law of God served as safeguards against the gods and paganism, their removal opened the door for the gods to come in unhindered… The nation [America] was left wide open to the subjugation and dominion of the gods.[17]

Once Baal's work of separating America from God had begun in earnest, other ancient gods, Asherah (Ishtar) and Molech, further transformed America into something unrecognizable. Almost every evil that has taken root in America since 1961 finds its characteristics rooted in Baal, Asherah, and Molech—what Cahn calls the dark trinity.[18]

What are the pagan beliefs that have changed our nation? Baal is "the other god, the substitute god … and was Israel's anti-God."[19] Today, culture is characterized by an anti-God spirit of the age. The one true God is loving and forgiving, promotes the truth that will set us free, and is the way to eternal life. But the cultural mindset is that the God of the Bible is probably a myth, and if He does exist, He and His followers are filled with hate.

Asherah is the goddess of sexuality, a seducer who mixes sex and intoxication, and her temple is a house of prostitution employing ritual sex acts. Asherah also employed sorcery and magic spells and gave oracles through her priests and priestesses.[20] As the characteristics of

Asherah manifest throughout culture, we would expect to see "ethics surrounding sexuality and marriage begin to erode."[21] Cahn explains:

> The sexual revolution was another dimension of the paganization of America and Western civilization. The values it represented were pagan values, and the sexuality was pagan sexuality. What was branded as the "new morality" was, in actuality, an old morality, an ancient morality, the morality of the gods.[22]

Asherah is also characterized by androgyny, transgenderism, the one who masculinizes women, feminizes men, and lures people into homosexuality. We have replaced the God who created sexuality between one man and one woman in marriage and created each person as a male or female with the pagan belief that LGBTQ is the way to freedom.[23]

Molech was also in defiance of God by demanding his worshipers sacrifice their children on his altar. Americans make this same sacrifice by aborting babies.[24] Cahn states:

> The paganization of America and Western civilization was now reaping its most bloody fruits. The once Christian civilization was now taking part in the most pagan of acts—the killing of its own children, their blood crying out to heaven ... There are few things that so invoke the judgment of God as the killing of little children.[25]

Some may argue that few, if any, Americans are worshiping Baal, Asherah, or Molech. But this assertion is immaterial. If our nation's practices reflect the values of these pagan gods, we are inviting dark spiritual forces to replace God, just as the ancient Israelites did, just as Jesus warned us not to do.

Occult Practices

Worshiping the one true God is also being replaced by the occult, that is, those who seek spiritual power through witchcraft and Satan worship. While this small minority has always lurked in the shadows, it is shocking to observe the growing acceptance of the occult today.

At the 2023 Grammy Awards, Sam Smith, a nonbinary (meaning he does not identify as a male or a female), sang his hit song *Unholy*, alongside superstar Kim Petras.[26] This highly sexualized performance was replete with evil ambiance, Satan personified by Smith, and a host of demonic entities dancing in some type of religious ritual culminating with cannibalism. His performance received wild applause and was viewed by tens of millions on YouTube.[27]

Judah, a pastor in a small town in Missouri, was recently troubled by a Witches, Warlocks, and Wizards Festival. In response, he created an alternative event across the street where Christian worship, Bible reading, preaching, and prayers to the one true God were offered.[28] Through this event and subsequent prayer, within a year, the primary organizer of this celebration was removed from office. In Judah's own words, he is thankful for how God has been honored in this community, yet is disturbed to see the occult's growing popularity throughout our nation.[29]

Replacing the God of the Bible with pagan gods and participating in the occult are central to why God will fight against a nation.

LGBTQ Freefall

Jordan, a popular high school teacher and athletic coach in the Midwest, did not have his 2023 teaching contract renewed. Why? Because he believes that God created each of his students as a male or a female. School administrators met with Jordan multiple times where he consistently explained why he could not support a transgender student's preferred pronouns. Jordan stood on God's truth and believed to do otherwise was to support a cultural lie. Jordan is taking legal action against the school district.

Similar accounts have put a chill in the air for teachers, Christian or not, who do not want to aid and abet cultural lies in their classrooms. Teaching in a cosmopolitan area, Jeff may leave the career he loves. Like many educators who are generally quiet about their faith, he is weighing how much longer he can remain under the radar while enduring the bombardment of godless LGBTQ ideologies that have overtaken his school.

Observing a similar shift in entertainment, Bible teacher and cultural commentator Timothy Zebell writes about the 2023 Oscar awards:

"I'm so excited!!" declared the LGBTQ activist Drew Gregory. "The Oscars this year are SO GAY!!" Indeed, this year's Academy Awards included an unreal number of LGBTQ-themed movies and documentaries, songs from queer icons, and LGBTQ directors, actors, and actresses … The big news of the night was the absolute domination of the movie *Everything Everywhere All at Once*. It was nominated for 11 awards and won 7 of them. For those who may be unfamiliar with the movie's plot, it revolves around an Asian immigrant mother who needs to learn that her lesbian daughter's girlfriend (who identifies as a man) should be introduced to grandpa, who also has to be taught to accept homosexuality and transgenderism as the new ways of the world.[30]

Unbelievably, the U.S. government published a statement stating that children as young as seven years old are able to discern what gender they prefer and should be able to decide for themselves if they want to begin puberty blockers.[31]

A national LGBTQ freefall will also provoke God's final judgment.

Fighting God

In his book *Letter to the American Church*, Eric Metaxas begins by stating that what America and the American church are facing is "almost unprecedented: the emergence of ideas and forces that ultimately are at war with God Himself." He goes on to say that rather than nationalistic, these forces are globalist in nature and rooted in atheistic Marxist ideology.[32] But why is Marxism with its various expressions—Socialism, Communism, neo-Liberalism, and Progressivism—evidence that America has crossed the line?

According to Marx and his followers, religion is the opiate of the people. It dulls the working man to his plight, which causes him to blindly serve capitalistic landowners and business owners. For most of my life, I only thought this position to be a difference of opinion. I thought it to be wrong, but I was unaware that the intent of Marxism is to destroy all forms of faith—the "opiate" of the people—often ruthlessly, to enforce socialism's control over the people.

All belief and devotion to anything other than the government is prohibited. It is the government, not God, that takes care of each person from cradle to grave. Washington D.C.'s massive debt and expansive social programs reveal how deeply America has ascribed to this ideal.

Behind the Soviet Union's Iron Curtain, Silvester Kremery, a Czechoslovakian physician, was eyed as a good socialist recruit until he gave his life to Christ. Sentenced to prison for his faith, where he was beaten and tortured 1951–64, Kremery was repeatedly deprived of sleep, food, and water. He was also forced to endure countless brainwashing sessions and months of isolation. On trial, the communists demanded that he renounce his faith. Kremery replied, "God gave me everything I have, and now that I face persecution because of Him and am called on to profess my faith in Him; should I now pretend I don't believe? Should I hide my faith? Should I deny Him?"[33] Kremery stood firm even though it meant ten additional unconscionable years of torture.

One Russian pastor, reflecting upon communism's persecution of the church, said, "Sixty years of terror and they were unable to get rid of the faith…Many didn't even have Bibles…whether you were at work in the factory, on the street, or anywhere else, everything was godless."[34]

While these are inspiring examples of those who stood firm in their faith, we must assess the degree to which America is following antiChrist, Marxist-socialist-progressive idealogy. This is another indicator that America is fighting against God, that is America has crossed the line.

Over the Line

Will God overlook the pagan and occult practices proliferating throughout our nation? Or how we have replaced His design for human sexuality and marriage with all things LGBTQ? Or how we are replacing faith in Him with the tenets of Marxist ideology?

Jonathan Cahn exclaims, "America is warring against her own foundations!" Is every American warring against God? No. A tipping point? Yes. Now that we have likely crossed the line, we have only begun to see what will happen when God chooses to war against us.

Our Response

We can learn vital lessons from David Wilkerson. First, regardless of how dark it looks or how certain we are that judgment is coming, we must continue to serve God wholeheartedly. We must warn the nation, seek God to revive His people, share the Good News as often as we can, and be influencers within our families and communities.

Anticipating severe judgment, Wilkerson chose to live sold out for Christ. In 1985, he said, "I intend to stay on the streets, preaching to junkies and harlots. I intend to write and distribute literature worldwide...Now that I know judgment is at the door, I work with even greater urgency."[35] And this is what he did until the Lord took him home.

Second, let's remember that our timeline of unfolding events is not always God's timeline. Wilkerson died forty years after coming to believe that devastating judgment was imminent—a judgment he never saw. In his case, and too many to count in my life, God's timeline proved to be much longer than anticipated.

In 2014, when God called us to launch *Forerunners of America*, I asked Him, "Are You sure about this? I don't think America will last long enough to establish a new ministry." Yet, here we are, warning the nation from a biblical perspective, calling people to repentance, and fasting and praying to see God revive the Church and take a widespread harvest of souls. Let's seize every opportunity to advance His Kingdom.

Third, Wilkerson serves as another example of a forerunner. He sought God, understood biblically what was taking place, observed what was taking place in culture, continued to seek God, heard from God, and resolutely warned the nation. He did all of this while producing the "much fruit" that Jesus said glorifies the Father (John 15:8). Inspired by Wilkerson, let's heed the words of Jesus to make every moment count while it is day. Night will surely come when no man can work (John 9:4), but it is still day!

• • •

Because it is still day, the balance of this book is devoted to responding in faith. In Part Two, we will seek to cultivate the qualities necessary to fulfill God's call on our lives. In Part Three, we will look at how to contend for the faith in the church, society, and government. It is to these topics that we must turn our attention to next.

PART 2
Fit for Service

SEEKING

Exult in his holy name; rejoice, you who worship the LORD. Search for the LORD and for his strength; continually seek him.

Psalm 105:3–4

Because we are called to contend for the faith, it is vital that we embrace a seeking God lifestyle (Chapter 7), stand firm against wickedness (Chapter 8), and be willing to sacrifice for Christ (Chapter 9). Let's start with what it means to seek God as a way of life.

Marked for Life

Not long after I had come to faith, I was invited to serve on a planning team to host a campus-wide outreach. It was designed to communicate the gospel through a multi-screen slide show accompanied by contemporary music. Steve, a freshman at St. Cloud State University, who had come to Christ as a high school student, was selected to provide leadership for the event. Even though the outreach was less than two months away, our weekly meetings always ended promptly in an hour. More surprising, the first forty-five minutes were spent in prayer, with only a few minutes remaining to brainstorm, plan, and organize. As a new believer, I was reluctant to speak up, but Steve's approach appeared to be destined for failure.

Steve scheduled a prayer meeting two days before the event. I thought, *instead of praying, maybe we should actually organize something.* To Steve's credit, we did have a 600-seat venue reserved, and the traveling slide show crew was scheduled to arrive a few hours before the outreach.

Sunday evening, we arrived for our final prayer time. This session was different because Steve had not mentioned an ending time. Only three of us showed up, and, in my opinion, certain failure loomed. Yet, Steve was in good spirits. Surprising, at least to me, when we began to pray, we sensed God drawing near, and our prayers deepened in focus and fervor. Maybe all was not lost. Or maybe God was drawing near because He felt sorry for us. I wasn't sure. We persevered.

The third participant was not part of our planning team. He was a forty-something member of the community who suddenly began to cry out for dead bones to live, meaning those on campus without the life of Christ to come to the outreach and find new life in Christ. His faith and passion were contagious, and we eagerly prayed for the walking dead to be born again.

This went on for quite some time, and suddenly, sensing God had heard us, we stopped interceding. We found ourselves standing firm on John's promise: "And we are confident that he hears us whenever we ask for anything that pleases him. And since we know he hears us when we make our requests, we also know that he will give us what we ask for" (1 John 5:14–15).

Walking home, I was stunned to realize that a full three hours had passed. I pondered, *why did it feel like our prayer time had only lasted ten minutes?* I also wondered how God was planning to answer our prayers. Something had changed. I had shifted from skepticism to believing we were about to see something miraculous.

Two days later, the outreach arrived. I walked into the auditorium filled to capacity with students, most of whom had no idea how to start a relationship with Jesus. The electricity in the air was palpable, suggesting God was up to something. The multimedia event started, and soon God's Spirit filled the room, and many of those spiritually dead students began to be stirred to come alive in Christ. Although there was no speaker or altar call—only a slide show accompanied by music—it was obvious God had come to seek and save the lost. It was powerful.

After the event, we all agreed that there was no human explanation for what happened. The presence and power of God had changed lives that evening, including mine. I was marked for life. I had witnessed that seeking God wholeheartedly matters and I would never be the same.

Having put my questions about Steve's leadership to rest, I swallowed my pride and thanked Steve for His godly, Spirit-led example. He knew what I did not: The key was not to rely on our best efforts but to seek God diligently and to rely completely on Him (Hebrews 11:1, 6). I also learned only to do what God directs, keeping organizational and planning efforts secondary to seeking Him. Indeed, it will be in the seeking when we will know what God wants us to do.

Seeking God is essential to see widespread change. The nation of Uganda provides such an example.

National Transformation

In 2009, my family traveled to the East African nation of Uganda to participate in a Christian conference hosted by indigenous leaders. We were excited to witness what God had been doing in this nation since the early 1980s.

Though experiencing jet lag on the first day, we decided to see the sights, including the headwaters of the Nile River. This was a memorable outing, but our tour guide became the highlight. This man and his wife had become Christians a few years earlier. Since then, they had preached the gospel in villages every weekend. He was only one of many Ugandans we met who lived contagious, faith-filled Christian lives.

Traveling to and from the conference each day, we saw numerous Christian business signs such as *My Redeemer Lives Laundromat*, and *With God All Things Are Possible Pharmacy*. These were visible manifestations that God was at work in a big way, but the conference itself revealed what was behind Uganda's transformation.

Before the first session, heartfelt, passionate prayers filled the auditorium for an entire hour. God's presence was apparent. No one looked at their watches, and it took the conference director a few minutes to corral these enthusiastic intercessors before he could start the session.

Various prayer gatherings throughout the week exposed a striking difference between the Ugandans' prayers and those from Western nations. The African prayers were heartfelt, full of faith, conviction, and power. When Westerners prayed, the prayers were sterile, theologically appropriate, careful, and … well … boring. If only Westerners had prayed, I believe most of us would have started to slip out the door for a cup of coffee.

Different Understanding

Ugandan Christians understand four principles of seeking God that most Western Christians do not. First, rather than offering up comforting platitudes or pseudo-spiritual statements, the Ugandans pray to draw near to God and to see God interact with them. James teaches, "Come close to God, and God will come close to you" (James 4:8). When God draws near, everything changes.

Second, Ugandans understand that God wants Christians to pray for His purposes to be accomplished, not simply to have their personal problems resolved (Matthew 6:10). Third, they understand from personal experience that prayer works; therefore, seeking God wholeheartedly through praise, thanksgiving, and intercession is foundational to all that they do (Psalm 17:6–7; Jeremiah 29:13). They do not simply put in time, but are on the edge of their seats dialoguing with the God of the universe. Fourth, Ugandans realize that their prayers need to be proportionate to the need of the hour. Ugandans detect evil in their nation and communities, and they seek God until wickedness is defeated and replaced with righteousness.

In America, we are witnessing an eruption of evil and, for the most part, life is simply business as usual. No urgency. No groundswell of moral outrage. No heartfelt concern fueling our prayer meetings—if prayer meetings exist at all.

Often, we would rather look to a political party or blame "all those sinful people out there" than direct our energy toward seeking

God through prayer. We are prone to believe that, given enough time, wickedness will magically disappear. All the while, we forget that eagerly seeking God, the One who loves us and created the universe, is the answer.

Like our brothers and sisters in Uganda, we must choose to draw near to God personally and as faith communities, make God's purposes our central prayer target, seek God wholeheartedly, and intercede proportionate to the need of the hour.

The Secret Place

This kind of prayer starts by seeking God in the secret place. King David is described as a man after God's own heart (1 Samuel 13:14; Acts 13:22). Threatened by military invasion, his parents' abandonment, and false witnesses (Psalm 27:2–3, 10–12), David declared:

> One thing I have asked from the Lord, that I shall seek:
> That I may dwell in the house of the Lord all the days of my life,
> To behold the beauty of the Lord
> And to meditate in His temple.
> For on the day of trouble He will conceal me in His tabernacle;
> He will hide me in the secret place of His tent;
> He will lift me up on a rock.
>
> Psalm 27:4–5 NASB

More than anything, David wanted to be close to God, know God, and live in His glorious presence. He knew that this place, this continuous heart posture before God, was also his place of protection from his enemies.

Again, we see his desire to know God more fully when he recounts, "When You said, 'Seek My face,' my heart said to You, 'I shall seek Your face, Lord'" (Psalm 27:8 NASB). Like a human relationship, we will not truly know God until we have seen His face, that is, come to know Him for who He is.

There is an urgent need to seek God on behalf of America, but first we must seek God to know Him, understand Him, love Him, and delight in His presence. This was God's invitation to David—the same invitation God offers us.

The secret place was also where Jesus met with His heavenly Father. He told the crowds it was there they, too, could meet with God:

> But as for you, when you pray, go into your inner room, close your door, and pray to your Father who is in secret; and your Father who sees what is done in secret will reward you.
>
> Matthew 6:6 NASB

Luke highlights, "But Jesus often withdrew to lonely places and prayed" (Luke 5:16). No doubt this was Jesus' secret place, the place where He met with His Father. The original language emphasizes that "often" means regular or frequent. To both David and Jesus, the secret place was an ongoing experience with the Father, which meant everything to them.

Especially Now

Seeking God, and specifically accepting Jesus' invitation into the secret place, has never been more important—at least not in America. We are living in the most dangerous season in our nation's history. Some may debate that the Civil War, The Great Depression, World War II, or the

Vietnam War were darker times in America. I disagree. As a nation, we have never rebelled against God like we are now. We have not been this spiritually deceived, confused, and morally compromised and, therefore, vulnerable to internal and external threats as we are today.

It is imperative to see that the cultural seeds we have sown have set us up for severe shakings and final judgment—all of which will cause the hearts of men and women to grow faint. Thus, we need to drink in passages like Psalm 91 until we see the secret place become a reality with the promises of God coming alive in our hearts.

The psalmist reveals that anyone can live in "the shelter of the Most High" and "in the shadow of the Almighty" (Psalm 91:1). However, living in these protected places is conditional. Each Christian must choose to live near God under His lordship, make Him the One we trust for protection, depend on Him as our source of all things, and choose to love Him above anyone or anything. Only then will God's protection be bestowed upon us (Psalm 91:1, 9–10, 14).

The Bible teaches that when a nation seeks God wholeheartedly, He responds by mitigating, delaying, or removing judgment. In America's case, I believe that averting judgment is no longer an option (see Chapter Six), and delaying God's wrath is possible but unlikely. Yet, if we will seek God wholeheartedly, I do believe in two hopeful outcomes.

First, in some churches and their surrounding communities, mitigation of God's wrath is in keeping with God's ways. In other words, the full brunt of God's fury poured out on every neighborhood, community, and city is not a foregone conclusion. In locations where a remnant is seeking God wholeheartedly, obeying Him, and crying out for God's purposes to be accomplished, America could go through a devastating shaking where there are pockets of His protection. This possibility echoes Psalm 91. Some have called these pockets places of refuge, or places of His presence.

It is vital that we seek God together. Addressing both Judah's imminent judgment and a future global judgment (Zephaniah 1:1–18), the prophet Zephaniah sounded the alarm:

> Gather together—yes, gather together,
> you shameless nation.
> Gather before judgment begins,
> before your time to repent is blown away like chaff.
> Act now, before the fierce fury of the Lord falls
> and the terrible day of the Lord's anger begins.
> Seek the Lord, all who are humble,
> and follow his commands.
> Seek to do what is right
> and to live humbly.
> Perhaps even yet the Lord will protect you—
> protect you from his anger on that day of destruction.
>
> Zephaniah 2:1–3

Second, barring the possibility that final judgment is next, greater shakings will likely create an atmosphere for a far greater harvest of souls—possibly the greatest harvest ever. Rather than giving up, it has never been more important to seek God's kingdom's purposes and His righteousness.

Let's Be Practical

Dr. Robert Wilken is a professor of Christian history at the University of Virginia. In his book, *The Spirit of Early Christian Thought: Seeking the Face of God*, he explains how important a seeking God lifestyle was to first-century Christians:

> The subtitle *Seeking the Face of God* is based on Psalm 105:4, in the Latin version, "Seek his face always" (Quaerite faciem eius semper) … More than any other passage in the Bible, it captures the spirit of early Christian thinking.[1]

Wilken asserts that more than martyrdom or miracles, the first-century church was characterized by seeking God wholeheartedly. He continues:

> As we come to know the God we seek, we discover that finding leads to further seeking. Maturity does not mean arriving, but "stretching out eagerly to what lies ahead" (Philippians 3:13). "Let us then," says Augustine, "seek as those who are going to find, and find as those who are going to go on seeking."
>
> When Augustine returns to the words of the Psalm, "Seek his face always," in the final prayer, he says, "I have sought you intellectually" and "I have argued much and toiled much." But then he adds, "Give me the strength to seek you," for as "you have caused yourself to be found," you have given me hope of finding you "more and more."[2]

Believers throughout history understood something—something that contemporary Western Christians have largely lost: Finding God in salvation is the beginning of seeking God, not the end. Matt Bennett, founder of Christian Union, a ministry to contend for the faith within influential secular institutions, explains, "Virtually every instance of the 130 times in the Bible that we see the phrase, 'seeking God,' it refers to believers seeking God, not unbelievers."

How then can we overcome the obstacles that are impeding us from living a seeking God lifestyle?

Helpful Rhythms

The prophet Daniel, holding a high position in the Babylonian government and later in the Persian Empire, prayed three times daily (Daniel 6:1–10). In addition to seeking God in the secret place, Peter and John prayed with other Christians daily at 3:00 p.m. (Acts 3:1). As we examine the Scriptures, whether individually or corporately, continuous rhythms of praying two to three times a day are apparent.

Specifically, to honor God and receive spiritual strength, early Christians prioritized seeking God every day in the morning (9:00 a.m.) and mid-day (3:00 p.m.), as seen in the book of Acts and substantiated in secondary sources.[3] This twice-daily pattern of seeking God originated from the Old Testament worship patterns and from creation itself (Exodus 29:38–41; 1 Chronicles 23:30; Luke 1:8–11). God designed the universe to indicate times and patterns for drawing close to Him (Genesis 1:14). The rising and setting of the sun signify that it is time to worship and seek God toward the beginning and end of each day. A case can be made from the New Testament that this is how God expects us to pray.[4]

Seeking God morning and evening was essential to the dramatic growth, strength, and spiritual vibrancy of the early church. They were full of the Spirit because they regularly took advantage of God's promise, "Draw near to God, and he will draw near to you" (James 4:8 ESV). The same was true when the church thrived throughout history, as it does in various locations around the world today. Morning and evening prayer is a foundational characteristic of God moving among His people.[5]

How should one seek God with this kind of fervor and frequency? Early Christians sought God twice each day, often with other believers, and for 30 minutes or more each time.[6] If we will spend significant time daily praising and thanking God, reading His Word, repenting of sin, and seeking His kingdom and righteousness in prayer, can you imagine the spiritual impact in your own life and on the church in America? It would be like the book of Acts all over again.[7]

No Legalism Allowed

Prayer rhythms and spiritual disciplines play a vital role in seeking God, hearing from God, and seeing God draw near. Even so, they must not become mere religious activities. Legalistic efforts where we attempt to earn our way into right standing with God, or try to cajole God to do something, repel God. David clarifies:

> You do not desire a sacrifice, or I would offer one.
> You do not want a burnt offering.
> The sacrifice you desire is a broken spirit.
> You will not reject a broken and repentant heart, O God.
> Look with favor on Zion and help her;
> rebuild the walls of Jerusalem.
>
> Psalm 51:16–18

What can guard us against seeking God legalistically? According to David, a humble repentant heart. It is from this place where David encountered God afresh and once again found the confidence to seek God to "rebuild the walls of Jerusalem."

Christian scholar, Dallas Willard (1935–2013), summarizes, "God is not against effort, but He is against earning." Indeed, obeying the commands of Scripture will require effort. Seeking God will be no different, but the resulting spiritual strength, joy, and changes in our families, churches, and communities will be worth it.

Once we begin to seek God wholeheartedly, other avenues of seeking and finding God will open up—even when we are spiritually dry.

Seeking God Out of Our Deficit

One day, while questioning my lukewarm praise, God prompted me in the most unexpected direction. He wanted me to praise Him from my spiritually dry heart! *Why would I do that, God? You know I'm driven to get things done, and praise doesn't come naturally even when things are going well, much less when I'm feeling empty.*

Even with this skeptical attitude, during my commute home, I mustered the obedience to praise God out of my deficit—that is my dry heart. I began to praise Him as the source of living water and the source of real life (John 7:37–39; Romans 8:6). It was an effort, but I did it. Choosing not to ask Him for anything, I continued to praise Him. Suddenly, He enveloped me in His presence! As my spirit quickly lifted, I praised Him more and more, and His glory enveloped me more and more. Arriving home, I realized that God changed me as I chose to praise Him in the very area in which I was struggling!

Since then, I've learned to praise God out of my deficit as a way of life: "Lord, I'm short on love for people today, but I praise You that You are love. I praise You that You love me and everyone else." As I speak these words in faith, His love fills my heart. Again, "Lord, I praise you that while I feel anxious about finances, You own the cattle on a thousand hills. You have more than I need or will ever need." Suddenly, my heart shifts from anxiety to trust, and so on.

Thanking and praising God has brought me near to Him and helped me live a seeking God lifestyle. Sometimes I thank and praise God quickly in the car, sometimes for longer seasons in the secret place, or during extended times with other Christians, almost always with great effect. I call this way of approaching God, praising God out of my deficit, which is one way I have learned to move from spiritual lack into the reality of Christ's abundance.

Hearts After God

"It is impossible to please God without faith. Anyone who wants to come to him must believe that God exists and that he rewards those who sincerely seek him" (Hebrews 11:6). Christian Union teaches seven keys of a seeking God lifestyle:

- Humbling one's self before God
- Fervent and frequent prayer
- Regular deep dives into Scripture
- Personal and corporate repentance
- Heartfelt obedience
- Living in Christian community
- Perseverance[8]

Special seasons of fasting are also an important aspect of seeking God—a spiritual discipline that can quickly take us deeper in the seven keys of a seeking God lifestyle.

My First Fast

My first fast was a three-day water-only fast. Before I started the fast, I wondered if, by the end of the last day, I would find myself lying in a hospital bed gasping for air. However, I was surprised to experience more energy and mental clarity when fasting than when I ate three meals a day. Indeed, I felt humbled, and my desire to read God's Word and obey it dramatically increased. God also showed me that it was not only what He wanted to do in me that was important, but also what He wanted to do through me.

During the second day of the fast, a friend and I entered one of the leading fraternities at the University of Wisconsin. I had previously spoken to sixty of these young men on how to start a relationship with Jesus Christ and had engaged in further discussions about the gospel with many of them individually. I enjoyed these conversations but had seen little fruit.

On this day, we walked into the fraternity and talked to one student after another about Christ and the Bible study I was about to start up. Surprisingly, most of these conversations took place on the second floor hallway because as soon as one person finished talking with us, another would immediately come up exuberantly asking questions. As we left the fraternity, my friend said, "Wow, Dave, those guys are going to rush you!"

That Bible study did happen, bearing fruit for years. One of these men is walking with Christ in the financial services industry, and another went to medical school and is serving overseas as a medical missionary. Lives were changed, and the impact for Christ is still happening today.

Launching Forerunners

In 2014, I went on an extended fast before launching *Forerunners of America*. Having just crossed the half-century mark, I did not want to miss what God was saying. Once again, while the seven keys to seeking God are always helpful, this special season of fasting took each of these keys further.

As I began my fast, I believed that God would guide and encourage me, but I had no expectation for anything profound to happen. However, by the third day, God was showing me so much in Scripture and in my life related to launching *Forerunners* that I started to journal. From that point, I found it necessary to journal every day until the fast ended. This was a special season when most of the seven keys—humbling myself, fervent and frequent prayer, a deeper dive into the Scriptures, heartfelt obedience, and perseverance—came together in a remarkable way that is still bearing fruit today.

Seeking God Together

I believe that in this desperate hour, God is calling Christians to seek Him wholeheartedly together through the seven keys, accompanied by special seasons of fasting. Isaiah reminds us that the window of God's patience and mercy will not stay open forever:

> Seek the Lord while you can find him. Call on him now while he is near. Let the wicked change their ways and banish the very thought of doing wrong. Let them turn to the Lord that he may have mercy on them. Yes, turn to our God, for he will forgive generously.
>
> Isaiah 55:6–7

Fit for Service

David is known for slaying Goliath, outlasting Saul, and numerous military victories. However, he was also known for playing his harp in the secret place, praising God, writing the psalms, and pleading for God's help. To be fit for service, no less will be required of us.

Day and night prayer rhythms, the seven keys to seeking God, praising God out of our deficit, and fasting will keep us close enough to God's heart to navigate the trouble that has arrived and the greater trouble that likely lies ahead.

• • •

Throughout the Bible, we see God's people facing all kinds of overwhelming situations. How can we be prepared for such challenges? Thankfully, we have the timeless example of the earliest New Testament forerunner. And it is to his ability to stand firm that we must turn our attention to next.

STANDING 8

If the godly give in to the wicked, it's like polluting a fountain or muddying a spring.

Proverbs 25:26

As John the Baptist prepared the way for Jesus, he modeled what it looks like to stand firm. His unwavering posture is a "now" message for us today.

Not Who We Would Expect

Though living in the wilderness, John saw multitudes of lives change without targeting population centers, employing marketing strategies, or preaching entertaining messages. Eating honey and locusts, wearing a camel hair outfit, and castigating the crowds, he was not interested in maintaining a respectable image. Then again, he did not come to be popular. He came to tell the truth.

Character Matters

American Christianity is a peculiar mix of Christian principles merged with personal preferences and obtaining whatever the world might offer. Living such diluted lives, we are too spiritually weak to stand firm, much less influence culture. Indeed, culture is influencing us.

Not so with John. Even his primary adversary, Herod, a tyrannical Gentile king, feared and protected John because he knew John to be "a righteous and holy man" (Mark 6:20 NIV). Regardless of circumstances, John stood firm and held Herod's respect.

Today, we excuse ourselves from living righteous and holy lives because it is too much effort and is often considered unattainable. Or we fear being rejected by those who may not approve of such a lifestyle. Why would we want to publicly stand firm on biblical principles when our employer, friends, and family might disagree with us? Do we really need the hassle? Both inside and outside of the church, we often simply go along to get along.

In contrast, the Bible teaches that righteousness and holiness are qualities that every believer should choose. John modeled these qualities and did not cave under pressure. Jonathan Edwards (1703–1758), pastor and leader during America's First Great Awakening, believed holiness to be the greatest thrill the human soul can experience. Author John Eldredge teaches that there is "utter relief" in choosing to live a holy life.[1] Paul instructed every believer to "Put on the new self, created to be like God in true righteousness and holiness" (Ephesians 4:24 NIV).

Even in the sexually charged city of Corinth, Paul exhorted believers to "Purify yourselves from everything that contaminates body and spirit, perfecting holiness out of reverence for God" (2 Corinthians 7:1 NIV). Peter called the body of Christ to purity, stating, "But now you must be holy in everything you do, just as God who chose you is holy. For the Scriptures say, 'You must be holy because I am holy'" (1 Peter 1:15–16).

As John demonstrated, and the New Testament teaches, holiness and righteousness are central to standing firm.

Courage Matters

Fear and timidity too often characterize American Christianity. We fear that teaching the full counsel of God will offend people. We fear if we uphold Jesus' claim as the only way to God, we will be labeled intolerant or xenophobes. We fear that if we affirm God's perspective on sexuality, we will be labeled as not inclusive and souring the lost to the gospel. We avoid the topic of creation because we fear scientists might come up with irrefutable evidence for evolution. Though God gave us His view on abortion long before Democrats and Republicans existed, we fear proclaiming the pro-life position will be viewed as politically motivated. We fear that asserting that God created marriage between one man and one woman for life, someone might unfriend us on Facebook.

Sadly, a lack of courage is most evident within the church. Leaders fear that preaching a culturally unacceptable message will reduce the Sunday morning attendance and the money that keeps everything running. These actions betray us, exposing where our hearts are at. Fear moves Christians and the church to capitulate to the culture.

Not so with John. John refused to allow the culture to dictate the conversation. He expected opposition and even greeted crowds of spiritual seekers and religious leaders alike: "You brood of vipers" (Matthew 3:7; Luke 3:7). More than a microaggression, John compared the people to poisonous snakes, spreading venom everywhere they went.

Calling out specific sins, the crowds were moved to repentance. John challenged the Jews to quit masking their hollow, hypocritical faith by vicariously claiming Abraham's faith. He told the middle and upper classes to turn from their self-centered lifestyles and get serious about helping the poor. He told tax collectors to quit padding their income by forcing citizens to pay more than required. He told Roman soldiers to stop extorting money. The love of money is the root of all evils, and John stood firm calling out this sin in numerous ways (Luke 3:8–14; 1 Timothy 6:10).

John fearlessly warned people that the ax of God's judgment was already laid at the root, proclaiming, "Every tree that does not bear good fruit will be chopped down and thrown into the fire" (Luke 3:9b). He also explained that the Messiah would "gather His wheat into the barn, but He will burn up the chaff with unquenchable fire" (Matthew 3:12 NASB).

John did not give these messages because he was angry. He wanted to expose self-deception and self-centeredness to help people awaken to the truth and set them free. Indeed, this approach was a courageous act of love because John was on a dual mission: liberate people from their personal bondages and prepare them to meet their King.

John's public confrontation of the people's sins eventually cost him his life. John called out King Herod for the many specific wrongs he had committed, which included marrying his brother's wife (Luke 3:19). Because of this offense, Herod imprisoned John. Later, John was executed at the behest of his stepdaughter, a deceit contrived by her mother (Mark 6:16–29). John spoke the truth despite the risks. Standing firm requires courage.

A "Now" Message Matters

Christian leaders often struggle to address key cultural issues, even though these are the very issues and offenses that are provoking God to judge our nation. The world recently experienced the COVID-19 pandemic. While the Bible identifies and warns of plagues and pestilence 115 times,[2] few pastors taught biblical truth about COVID's spiritual significance and the church's role in remedying the pandemic. Leaders often responded to COVID by replacing God's message with instructions on social distancing, wearing masks, vaccines, and personal hygiene tips.

Not so with John. Anticipating Christ's imminent public life and ministry, John declared God's "now" message to the people: "The Messiah is about to be revealed! Repent!" Like the men of Issachar, John understood the times and knew what to do (1 Chronicles 12:32). Pastor and author A.W. Tozer (1897–1963) urged leaders in his day to give God's "now" message:

> What God says to His church at any given period depends altogether upon her moral and spiritual condition and upon the spiritual need of the hour. Religious leaders who continue mechanically to expound the Scriptures without regard to the current religious situation are no better than the scribes and lawyers of Jesus' day who faithfully parroted the Law without the remotest notion of what was going on around them … The prophets never made that mistake nor wasted their efforts in that manner. They invariably spoke to the condition of the people of their times.[3]

What can we learn from John's approach and Tozer's insight? Rather than neglecting to speak timely exhortations due to fear of controversy, we must stand firm proclaiming God's "now" message.

Numbers Do *Not* Matter

In American Christianity, success is often measured by the size of the crowd. If the church is not growing, it is assumed that the church is doing something wrong. Therefore, leaders shrink back from controversial topics that will not produce numerical growth. The greatest sin within the church is not pornography, adultery, or replacing love for Jesus with love of the world. The greatest "sin" is declining attendance.

Rather than speaking God's truth, our tendency is to nuance controversial subjects to make them more palatable, or avoid them altogether. It is hard to find a biblical example of this approach, but in America this is the air we breathe.

Not so with John. Numbers, fame, crowds, and budgets had no hold on him, which allowed him to stand firm, confronting people—including Herod—on every topic. He was free from ecclesiastical posturing, cultural expectations, and peer pressure. He preached before an audience of One. To stand firm, we, too, will need to boldly speak the truth, just as John did, regardless of the response.

Humility Matters

Son of a respected priest with auspicious qualifications, conditions were ripe for John to move into an influential leadership position. However, John shunned prestige, embracing an austere, non-conformist lifestyle, stating he was nothing more than "a voice shouting in the wilderness" (John 1:23).

At the height of his ministry, John was likely preaching to and baptizing hundreds of people daily. With such a top-performing ministry, he might have felt well-qualified to baptize the Messiah. Yet when Jesus sought him to be baptized, John responded, "I need to be baptized by you, and do you come to me?" (Matthew 3:14 NIV). Rather than relishing the opportunity, John acknowledged his own spiritual need.

When confronted with his fading ministry, John simply replied, "No one can receive anything unless God gives it from heaven" (John

3:27). It was this same humility that led him to exclaim, "I am filled with joy for His success. He [Jesus] must become greater and greater, and I must become less and less" (John 3:29b–30).

Moreover, John was not motivated to expand his following nor grow his subscribers. John understood that it was more important for people to follow Jesus than it was for him to maintain his following. Therefore, he simply did what every forerunner should do: Point people to Jesus to assist Him in advancing His kingdom.

Will we follow the American ministry model of attracting crowds, expanding staff, constructing buildings, and expanding budgets, or will we simply influence those God puts before us for as long as God desires, and then, in humility, like John, step aside?

A Place of Strength

Our place of strength to stand firm comes from trusting in God's promises, understanding our identity in Christ, and relying on God's power.

Empowering Promises

In light of what we are facing in America, it has never been more important for Christians to know and rely upon the promises of God. Some empowering promises to start with are:

- "Greater is He who is in you [the Holy Spirit] than he [Satan] who is in the world" (1 John 4:4 NASB).
- "Seek first His kingdom and his righteousness and all these things [all that is needed in life] will be added to you" (Matthew 6:33 NASB).

- "The Lord will withhold no good thing from those who do what is right" (Psalm 84:11).
- "The LORD keeps watch over you as you come and go, both now and forever" (Psalm 121:8).
- "I will never fail you. I will never abandon you" (Hebrews 13:5).
- "I have given you authority to trample on snakes and scorpions [evil spirits] and to overcome all the power of the enemy; nothing will harm you" (Luke 10:19 NIV).

Adding to these promises and walking in them daily is vital and will become increasingly important in the days ahead.

Identity

Who we are in Christ is equally important. When we came to faith in Jesus, God declared that we are sons and daughters adopted into His family, new creations, forgiven of everything, and have the mind of Christ.[4] Also, we have crossed from death to life, are reconciled to God, His ambassadors to a lost world, and are "more than conquerors."[5]

It is vital we dwell on these truths and reject the notion that we are not good enough. God has accepted us as His own, lives in us, and, in Christ, has made us more than good enough to walk through what is here now and what is ahead.

Relying on God's Power

When standing firm, we must rely on God to intervene. Once again, we look to John, who came in "the spirit and power of Elijah" (Matthew 11:14; Luke 1:17).

Both John and Elijah were righteous men who followed God into great exploits with the Spirit's anointing. Elijah stood firm, relying on God, as he took on 850 prophets of Baal and Asherah and saw the crowd turn and cry out to the one true God (1 Kings 18:36–39). Similarly, John confronted religious leaders and challenged those who came to him from Jerusalem, all Judea, and all around the Jordan River to repent (Matthew 3:5–10).

Both Elijah and John opposed political figures: Elijah confronted King Ahab and Queen Jezebel, whereas John opposed King Herod and Herodias. Both stood their ground in the face of opposition. Both had God's "now" message, which exposed people's hearts. Both called people to believe in and follow the one true God.

Clearly, John came in the spirit of Elijah, but what about coming in Elijah's power—a power that came from God? Elijah saw the dead raised, weather patterns change, fire fall from heaven, and miraculous provision. If John came in the power of Elijah, how come these miracles are not attributed to him?

While Elijah and John walked equally in God's power, the Spirit's anointing manifested in them differently. In John's ministry, God's power was provided primarily to see the conviction of sin and the repentance of multitudes of people. In Elijah's ministry, God's power manifested in several spectacular miracles. In both cases, it was the same power coming from the same God. Once Jesus' ministry began, God's powerful work, portrayed in John and Elijah's ministries, found full expression in one person—the Son of God.

Like Elijah and John, relying on God's intervention will strengthen us to stand firm to carry out God's purposes.

Once the Holy Spirit was given at Pentecost to indwell every believer, we see God intervening continuously. Before Pentecost, the disciples were plagued with doubt and fear. Even when Jesus needed them most, they ran (Matthew 26:56). After the outpouring of the

Holy Spirit, they stood firm preaching the gospel, saw the miraculous on numerous occasions, and doubt was replaced with the courage to suffer and die for what they believed. Something changed—and that something was the indwelling, filling, and reliance upon the Holy Spirit.

What About Us?

Is there any admired biblical figure who did not stand firm against evil? If not, why would we think that Christians in America will get a pass? Are we aware of any areas where God is calling us to stand publicly against evil? Were we confronted by evil? Did we cave by staying silent or denying Christ? Do we need to repent of our cowardice?

Are we fooling ourselves into believing that we are standing firm when our actions speak otherwise? If so, what a curious faith we have created. It is a version of Christianity Jesus would not recognize—a version where Christians do not need to stand publicly. A version where personal comfort and appearance are our primary concerns. Curious indeed.

Church Culture

Paul Horrocks, author and host of the Biblical Courage podcast, explains how vital it is to stand firm. After twenty years of searching for fulfillment in the world, he came back to church and noticed a dramatic shift. Growing up in a church with his dad as the pastor, he had observed that when culture and the Bible were in conflict, churchgoers went with the Bible. "It's not that they didn't have sin issues," Horrocks explains, "but their worldview was based on the Bible and that the Bible was right and the culture was wrong."[6]

Returning to the church later in life, he noticed that church attenders were siding with culture. They almost seemed to be celebrating their "enlightenment." Horrocks also realized that this shift was not an exception—the church siding with culture had become a widespread reality.

He observed that pastors rarely talked about moral issues, especially sexual compromise, while the outside world was bombarding people with deviant sexual messaging ten to twenty times a day. Horrocks concludes, "If the church is only going to talk about these issues once a year, who is going to win this battle?"[7]

The necessity for church leadership to stand firm biblically on every issue is only one important aspect of the way forward. The call for all Christians is to stand firm within our families, among our friends, neighbors, and those with whom we work.

Standing Firm

A father of five, Chris was in sales and his family's only source of income. One day his boss, the business owner, announced they would start overbilling clients to increase the bottom line. Once the boss left the room, the sales team looked to Chris to see if his well-known Christian faith was real. They wanted to see if Chris would stand or cave to the pressure of needing a paycheck.

Seeking the Lord with his wife that evening, Chris knew what he had to do. The next day, he told the owner that he wanted to work for him because he had a great product at a fair price, but this new billing practice would undermine it all. On the spot, standing firm on his convictions and trusting God would provide for his family, Chris resigned.

Suddenly and unexpectedly, the owner reversed the billing practice and Chris stayed at the company. God also protected Chris' Christian witness with the sales team. Moreover, his coworkers were blessed by not having to comply with a deceptive billing practice.[8]

Similar to Chris, will we stand firm, doing what is right in God's eyes under pressure?

Fit for Service

Like John the Baptist, we must choose character over compromise, courage over cowardice, a "now" message over entertaining messages, faithfulness over fame, and humility over hubris. Standing firm will not be easy. If it were, Christians everywhere would be doing it. Horrocks exhorts, "When we look at Jesus' life and message, we should not tell people the Christian life is easy. We should tell them it is hard."[9] Trusting God's promises, living out our identity in Christ, and relying on God's power, we must stand firm against wickedness and disciple others to do the same.

• • •

However, there is a great cost of admission to join the society of those who stand firm. It is to this topic that we must turn our attention to next.

SUFFERING

> *Only let your manner of life be worthy of the gospel of Christ, so that ... I may hear of you that you are standing firm in one spirit, with one mind striving side by side for the faith of the gospel, and not frightened in anything by your opponents ... For it has been granted to you that for the sake of Christ you should not only believe in him but also suffer for his sake.*
>
> Philippians 1:27–29 ESV

According to Paul, standing firm, striving together for the faith, facing opposition, and suffering are central to the Christian life. This contending mindset can be hard for American Christians to grasp because we have enjoyed God's blessings for so long.

Suffering Today

Too often, we believe that if anything extraordinarily difficult takes place in our nation or world, we will be long gone, raptured into heaven. However, whether one believes in a pre-, mid-, or post-tribulation rapture, there is plenty of evidence that we are already facing opposition with much greater challenges ahead.

To suggest otherwise not only contradicts the Bible—Paul gave the above admonition for Christians to follow in every generation—but also minimizes the current suffering of Christians around the world. Muslims who become followers of Jesus are often tracked down by authorities and required to choose between "paying a weekly conversion fee no one can conceivably afford, renounce Christ, or be killed."[1] Even in recent years in Uganda, which is 84% Christian, Muslim extremists have beaten, starved, and killed many who converted from Islam to Christianity.[2]

Believers in communist nations, such as China and North Korea, endure brutal persecution. Christians in India are often tormented, even killed, by Hindu zealots. In the last thirty years, the number of countries where Christians suffer high or extreme levels of persecution has almost doubled, now totaling seventy-six.[3] None of these Christians were saved from intense suffering through a timely rapture.

Letter to the West

Corrie ten Boom (1892–1983) and her sister Betsie (1885–1944) were captured and put in Nazi concentration camps because of their efforts to save Jews in Holland during World War II. Betsie died at Ravensbruck prison, an exceptionally cruel concentration camp where prisoners were sent to die. However, Corrie was released because of an "error" made by the camp administration.

Thirty years later, ministering in numerous countries, Corrie was compelled to write the following letter to the Western Church:

> There are some among us teaching there will be no tribulation, that the Christians will be able to escape all this. These are the false

teachers that Jesus was warning us to expect in the latter days. Most of them have little knowledge of what is already going on across the world. I have been in countries where the saints are already suffering terrible persecution.

In China, the Christians were told, "Don't worry, before the tribulation comes you will be translated – raptured." Then came a terrible persecution. Millions of Christians were tortured to death. Later I heard a Bishop from China say, sadly,

> We have failed. We should have made the people strong for persecution, rather than telling them Jesus would come first. Tell the people how to be strong in times of persecution, how to stand when the tribulation comes, to stand and not faint.

I feel I have a divine mandate to go and tell the people of this world that it is possible to be strong in the Lord Jesus Christ. We are in training for the tribulation, but more than sixty percent of the Body of Christ across the world has already entered into the tribulation. There is no way to escape it.

We [in the West] are next.[4]

Fifty years ago, Corrie gave this forerunner message, a warning that American Christians must heed today: We will suffer for our faith, and we need to prepare.

Peter's Perspective

Peter appeals to every Christian: "Since Christ suffered physical pain, you must arm yourselves with the same attitude he had, and be ready to suffer, too. For if you have suffered physically for Christ, you have finished with sin" (1 Peter 4:1). In other words, Jesus is not an exception. He is our example. Peter is also teaching that if we make the greater decision to physically suffer for Christ, we will naturally make the easier decision not to sin.

Peter further tells us not to be surprised when persecution comes but to rejoice because suffering for Jesus is a sign that we are blessed by God. Also, because we have been found worthy to suffer, we will experience God's glorious presence and be overjoyed at Jesus' return (1 Peter 4:12–16). This reflects Jesus' call to follow God no matter the cost:

> God blesses those who are persecuted for doing right, for the Kingdom of Heaven is theirs. God blesses you when people mock you and persecute you and lie about you and say all sorts of evil things against you because you are my followers. Be happy about it! Be very glad! For a great reward awaits you in heaven. And remember, the ancient prophets were persecuted in the same way.
>
> Matthew 5:10–12

Paul's Perspective

When Paul wrote the book of Philippians, he was sitting in jail debating whether he should live or die. He was not pondering imminent death from old age or illness, but rather dying due to living courageously for Christ:

> For I fully expect and hope that I will never be ashamed, but that I will continue to be bold for Christ, as I have been in the past. And I trust that my life will bring honor to Christ, whether I live or die. For to me, living means living for Christ, and dying is even better. But if I live, I can do more fruitful work for Christ. So I really don't know which is better. I'm torn between two desires: I long to go

and be with Christ, which would be far better for me. But for your sakes, it is better that I continue to live.

Philippians 1:20–24

Paul knew he could die because of proclaiming Christ, yet he did not dread such an outcome. He joyfully anticipated being with Jesus! This hope was central to his enthusiastic attitude throughout this letter:

> Yes, everything else is worthless when compared with the infinite value of knowing Christ Jesus my Lord. For his sake I have discarded everything else, counting it all as garbage, so that I could gain Christ and become one with him … I want to know Christ and experience the mighty power that raised him from the dead. I want to suffer with him, sharing in his death, so that one way or another I will experience the resurrection from the dead!

Philippians 3:8–11

Later, when Paul was urged by his friends, disciples, and the prophet Agabus not to go to Jerusalem because certain persecution awaited him, he said, "Why all this weeping? You are breaking my heart! I am ready not only to be jailed at Jerusalem but even to die for the sake of the Lord Jesus" (Acts 21:13).

Coming Persecution

It is easy to assume these passages were written to address extreme circumstances faced by first-century Christians. In the 21st century, we assume that Christians, especially in America, will enjoy relatively stable lives until we die or are raptured. However, if we stop to notice, we observe Christians facing numerous challenges around the world now with every indication that much greater difficulty is ahead, including in America.

Received through a vision, the prophet Daniel describes a terrifying beast with global influence that will wage war against God's people and "wear down the saints" before Jesus returns (Daniel 7:25 NASB). This beast, the fourth in Daniel's vision, identified as "terrifying" three times, is an evil empire that literally takes over the world.

How do we know this? Daniel tells us: "This fourth beast is the fourth world power that will rule the earth. It will be different from all the others. It will devour the whole world, trampling and crushing everything in its path" (Daniel 7:23).

This global totalitarian government will not gain control overnight. In my view, the Great Tribulation (the final seven-year period before Jesus' second coming) has not begun, but this beastly system is taking shape now through international alliances led by those who seek a global government. Addressed in Chapter Three, various globalists and their organizations, such as the World Economic Forum, deceive the populace to follow their dangerous path into globalism.

This emerging beast system provides a clear trajectory to the seemingly impossible fulfillment of Daniel's vision—a vision also described by John (see Revelation 13:1–8). Here are but a few of the characteristics of Daniel's terrifying beast we see emerging throughout the world today.

Surveillance Society

Monitoring and controlling people are top priorities for those who are ambitiously creating this global totalitarian empire. Therefore, a comprehensive surveillance system must be in place, which is now evolving at a dizzying speed.

Suffering

In 2004, with microchip technology already embedded and tracking over a million pets, RFID (Radio Frequency Identification) chips received FDA approval to be implanted in humans. From that moment, concerns were raised, not about finding lost pets or people, but about the ability of the government to track the citizenry's movements. Concerns were also raised about a person's most private information, including medical records being stored on chips and potentially accessed by hackers.[5]

Revealing indeed, the Bible does not warn us about a rogue individual sitting in his apartment in Chicago retrieving our most personal information stored on a chip implant, but Daniel does warn us of a global government—the fourth beast—using this type of technology to control every person on earth.

In his 2022 article, *Microchips in Humans: Consumer-friendly App or New Frontier in Surveillance*, an expert in cybersecurity, Ahmed Banafa writes:

> People are *voluntarily* having these chips—technically known as "radio frequency identification chips" (RFIDs)—injected under their skin, because these microscopic chips of silicon allow them to pay for purchases at a brick and mortar store just by hovering their hand over a scanner at a checkout counter, entirely skipping the use of any kind of a credit card, debit card, or cell phone app ... The underlying driver [to use RFID chips] has always been the goal of expanding the abilities and powers of humans by making certain tasks easier and less time-consuming.
>
> Consequently, such consumer technology can look like the next logical step... But on second glance, the insertion of identifying microchips in humans would also seem to bear the seeds of a particularly intrusive form of surveillance, especially at a time

when authorities in some parts of the world have been forcibly collecting DNA and other biological data—including blood samples, fingerprints, voice recordings, iris scans, and other unique identifiers—from all their citizens, in an extreme form of the surveillance state.[6]

The G20 is an international governance group comprised of twenty countries, including the United States. In a 2023 meeting, the G20 discussed the worldwide implementation of digital IDs, digital records, and digital currencies.[7] Once this digitized data is stored on a chip and implanted, the ability for Daniel's terrifying beast to control every person on the planet will be a reality.

Social Scoring

Well beyond a FICO credit score, the social scoring of each citizen is another step toward controlling people. Citizens will be increasingly pressured to follow the government's positions on everything from same-sex marriage to receiving forced vaccines to submitting to censorship policies. If someone chooses not to support LGBTQ lifestyles or speaks out against government policies, one's social score will plummet, along with one's freedom.

In 2018, CBS News reported that Chinese citizens were well on their way to being controlled through social scoring:

> When Liu Hu recently tried to book a flight, he was told he was banned from flying because he was on the list of untrustworthy people. Liu is a journalist who was ordered by a court to apologize for a series of tweets he wrote and was then told his apology was insincere.
>
> "I can't buy property. My child can't go to a private school," he said. "You feel you're being controlled … all the time."[8]

Lest we assume that social scoring is an extreme surveillance measure only practiced by communist China, Business Wire, a Berkshire Hathaway subsidiary, alerted investors to the enormous potential of investing in companies that will provide the infrastructure for social scoring worldwide. Almost every nation in the world is advocating citizen surveillance, allegedly to effectively respond to pandemics, improve homeland security, and save the planet through indoor climate control. That's right, Daniel's beast would like to set your thermostat for you. Based on market research, social scoring infrastructure will be a $16 billion global industry by 2026.[9]

If this was not enough to inspire potential investors to put their money into social scoring infrastructure, Business Wire lists 37 corporations that have already jumped on board. These include Amazon, Google, Facebook, Apple, IBM, Honeywell, Samsung, and Sony.[10] Clearly, whatever is happening is not being driven by communist countries alone but appears to be a global phenomenon, just as the books of Daniel and Revelation predicted thousands of years ago.

Digital Currency

A global empire bent on total control will likely use Central Bank Digital Currencies (CBDC's) to monitor every dollar a person spends and receives. Controlling the populace is far easier when the looming threat of the government turning off one's bank account exists.

One of the 168,000 practicing osteopathic physicians in the U.S., Dr. Joseph Mercola, saw his business bank accounts, along with his CEO and CFO's personal bank accounts—including their spouses and kids' accounts—closed by Chase Bank in July 2023. After confusion about the reason for Chase closing these accounts, a Chase spokesperson wrote that Mercola's business had "been the subject of regulatory scrutiny by the Federal government ... for engaging in illegal activity relating to the marketing and sale of consumer products." Confusion persisted because the only marketing and sale of products that had been in question had been resolved two years prior.[11]

At that time, the FDA sent a warning letter alleging that Dr. Mercola's support for the use of vitamins C and D, quercetin, and pterostilbene to mitigate, prevent, and treat COVID-19 was in violation of the Federal Food, Drug, and Cosmetic Act.[12] However, these protocols were supported by research, scientific data, and clinical results.

Mercola explains, "A warning letter is not proof of illegal activity. It's an accusation. We responded to the FDA's letter and no further action was ever taken, because we had not, in fact, violated the law." What, then, was the reason for Chase de-banking him, his colleagues, and their families? Mercola continues:

> The most likely reason appears to be the bank's relationships to the technocratic control network that is trying to usher in a one world totalitarian government. Since our de-banking, we've discovered that Chase Bank has several connections to entities that are pushing the Orwellian dystopia that is The Great Reset, both domestically and internationally.[13]

In a forerunner-esque article, Daniel Payne highlights the Canadian trucker protests against COVID vaccine mandates in 2022 ... and why Americans need to wake up:

> The Canadian government has invoked the National Emergencies Act, which confers upon government ministers the power to freeze the bank accounts of people protesting against the government itself, to suspend their right to public assembly, to limit their

movements, to seize property, and to compel workers to assist the government in breaking up protests …

The government will also require insurance companies to refuse to cover any vehicles used during blockade protests. Police will be working with banks to identify and punish protesters. Credit card companies will be required to report any protest activity to the government.

All of this is occurring because a relatively small but determined contingency of Canadian citizens did not want to be forced to take the COVID vaccine. For that, the Canadian government has imbued itself with what George Orwell called "omnipresent and omnipotent" powers: Canadian officials can essentially do whatever they want, with no restrictions, for whatever reason they deem.

It is time to start preparing for this eventuality in the United States. You might argue: "It would never happen here." Of course it could. What would stop it? The would-be tyrants currently in charge of our federal government are no less ruthless and no more inhibited than those in charge of Canada's; they are looking at Justin Trudeau right now with a mixture of admiration and envy. They want what he has, and if given the chance, they will take it.

To be sure, our Constitution is meant to constrain this type of tyranny, but at present it can only do so modestly. A century of bad court decisions and the ongoing erosion of constitutional norms have rendered the Bill of Rights increasingly notional rather than actual. There would be little to stop a truly determined administration from seizing the kinds of powers now held by Trudeau.[14]

If we are observing the erosion of constitutional rights in first-world nations like Canada and America, what nation is not presently encountering the beast's impulses? Prophesied in Revelation, the exact method to stop the ability of Christians to "buy or sell" is now coming into focus (Revelation 13:17). CBDCs will almost certainly be the mechanism by which this is accomplished.

An Unfolding Reality

The policies and infrastructure of Daniel's terrifying beast are already being put in place. What is the fate of those who choose not to aid and abet this global totalitarian government? If we choose to stand firm in Christ and strive together for the gospel, we should expect persecution. John gives this forerunner message to Christians who are alive at the time of the emerging beast system: "This means that God's holy people must endure persecution patiently and remain faithful" (Revelation 13:10; 14:12).

Sources

In addition to Daniel's prophesied global control of people and the wearing down of the saints, America is currently witnessing the emergence of three sources of persecution.

Culture of Lies

After God sent final judgment to Israel in 721 B.C., He declared that He was ready and willing to help Judah. He ultimately chose not to, and Isaiah addressed why God was about to withhold His favor: "Your wrongdoings have caused a separation between you and your God, and your sins have hidden *His* face from you so that He does not hear" (Isaiah 59:2 NASB). Judah was in conflict with God.

Like America today, central to Judah's apostasy was a culture of lies. Isaiah continues: "Your lips are full of lies, and your mouth spews corruption"; "No one cares about being fair and honest, the people's lawsuits are based on lies"; "Our courts oppose the righteous, and justice is nowhere to be found"; "Truth stumbles in the streets, and honesty has been outlawed" (Isaiah 59:3–14). Sound familiar?

Living in this environment is distressing enough, but it gets worse: "Yes, truth is gone, and anyone who renounces evil is attacked" (Isaiah 59:15). In other words, if you deviate from cultural lies and corruption, wicked people will come after you.

America's COVID crisis provides revealing examples of how good and honest people can become the prey. Practicing physician and former Minnesota state senator Dr. Scott Jensen was instructed by CDC officials and other medical professionals to lie by listing COVID as a primary, rather than contributing, cause of death on patient death certificates.

Sounding the alarm to the broader public and directly to Minnesota's medical board, Jensen soon found himself in the crosshairs of the healthcare establishment with his qualifications to practice medicine under attack. Faced with an onslaught of threats due to his whistleblowing, Jensen felt compelled to stand his ground:

> A real underlying question for me is why didn't I just keep my mouth shut? And ultimately, I think what happened was through the recurrent investigations that I was put through, I think that I became somewhat morally protected. I felt like the words of Esther 4:14—have you considered you're in the position you're in "for such a time as this"—really rang true in my life.
>
> I had access to information people didn't have. I absolutely was doing my ... due diligence. I was reading two, three, four hours a day, trying to keep current on all the issues going on with the Minnesota Senate and the COVID pandemic worldwide, and trying to hold my family together as well. In the end, I felt that

I was absolutely entrusted to be a voice to watch out for those encroachments on our liberties to say, "No! We're not going to let government expand willy-nilly just because they can."[15]

Jensen was willing to stand for the truth and do what was right in God's eyes regardless of the outcome, but it came at a cost.

Gail MaCrae was a patient care nurse in a California hospital at the height of COVID. She worked at a facility that did not see the alarming death count and beleaguered emergency rooms reported by the media. MaCrae first became concerned by the fact that patient families could not be at their loved one's side, with appropriate precautions, for what simply seemed more like a new flu strain than a death sentence.[16]

She then became troubled by what appeared to be financially motivated COVID diagnoses driving clinical care decisions. Her concerns came to a head over the dangerous misinformation asserting that the COVID vaccines were safe and effective. This was the issue that finally pushed her to confront her hospital's leadership, ultimately costing MaCrae her job. She observed first-hand that the vaccine was not protecting people but was responsible for increasing hospitalizations, an alarming reality few media outlets reported.[17]

MaCrae remains inspired to expose the widespread lies associated with virtually every aspect of the COVID crisis:

> I want to try and inspire courage in the world around us. There seems to be the trend I have seen the last two-three years now is ... a lot of practitioners with very little courage.[18]

A culture of lies matters. Therefore, the truth on every topic matters. Yet, there is a price to be paid when fighting lies. Scott Jensen and Gail MaCrae stood firm and willingly sacrificed. In Isaiah's words, they became the prey. Staying silent to keep the peace is no longer an option.

Are you willing to stand firm and speak the truth, even if it means becoming the prey?

Cultural Backlash

While explaining that God created each human as either male or female (Genesis 1:27), pastor emeritus of Moody Church in Chicago, Erwin Lutzer, invoked science, stating: "If you are a man, you will always have male chromosomes; if you are woman, you will always have female chromosomes. Every cell in your body is programmed to be male or female."[19] From a biblical or at least scientific perspective, based on its own merits, this conclusion should be able to be calmly weighed by Christians and the irreligious alike.

However, making such statements is increasingly met with vitriol. When Nebraska introduced legislation to ban questionable measures such as puberty blockers, hormone treatment, and sex change operations, Senator Machaela Cavanaugh threatened, "I will burn this session to the ground over this bill." She added, "If this legislature collectively decides that legislating hate against children is our priority, then I am going to make it painful—painful for everyone."[20] That's right. If we disagree with those who support gender fluidity—whether basing our position on the Bible, science, or common sense—we will be accused of hating children and inciting legislators to burn the house down.

A groundswell of Americans appear to agree with this militant view. In Murfreesboro, Tennessee, one protester held a sign reading "TRANS GIRLS NEED GUNS." Trans activists have also posted photos online wearing T-shirts that read "trans rights ... or else," alongside images of AK-47s, M-16s, and other firearms.[21] This mentality is similar to the cultural mindset in Sodom, where the LGBTQ community surrounded Lot's house to force their demands on his guests (Genesis 19:4–9).

In a heartbreaking turn of events, on March 27, 2023, Audrey Hale, a transitioning male, walked into The Covenant School near Nashville and killed three teachers and three students. As expected, there was an outpouring of love and prayers for the families of the six deceased. Yet, social media lit up, blaming Christians for the killer's actions, claiming that those at this Christian school represented transgender hate and had incited the killings.

This backlash against Christians is not simply coming from a fringe group of social media keyboard warriors. Four days after the school shooting in Tennessee, President Joe Biden proclaimed March 31 as the annual "Transgender Day of Visibility," stating:

> Today, we show millions of transgender and nonbinary Americans that we see them, that they belong, and they should be treated with dignity and respect. Their courage has given countless others strength, but no one should have to be brave just to be themselves.[22]

Painting transgenders as a helpless, victimized community, he also called on Americans to stand against those who hold traditional values:

> Together, we also have to keep challenging the hundreds of hateful state laws that have been introduced across the country, making sure every child knows that they are made in the image of God, that they are loved, and that we are standing up for them ... And to work toward eliminating violence and discrimination against all transgender, gender nonconforming, and nonbinary people."[23]

Once again, inflammatory verbiage was employed against people who hold the biblical position on gender. In this case, the President of the United States attempted to promote love toward the transgender community by urging the nation to fight against "hateful state laws." Yet, these laws were written to protect kids from mutilating their bodies through life-altering surgeries. The biblical view of fixed genders, a gender binary, is increasingly equated with discrimination. In light of our nation's trajectory, we should expect more—not less—cultural backlash when advocating similar biblical positions.

Government Overreach

The problem with government overreach is that the government overreaches. Centralized power undermines individual freedoms and eventually creates a climate for persecution. When this happens, Christians are ridiculed, attacked, marginalized, imprisoned, ostracized, and die. This is the path America is taking.

The book of Daniel gives two examples of God's people standing firm when facing government overreach. First, Daniel recounts the Babylonian government's mandate to worship a ninety-foot statue of the emperor.

Daniel records Shadrach, Meshach, and Abednego being thrown into a fiery furnace for refusing to obey the king's edict to bend their knees to him as the ultimate sovereign. In the moment of truth, they remained standing while everyone else literally bowed to political pressure. Summoned to answer for their defiant actions, they replied:

> O Nebuchadnezzar, we do not need to defend ourselves before you. If we are thrown into the blazing furnace, the God whom we serve is able to save us. He will rescue us from your power, Your Majesty. But even if he doesn't, we want to make it clear to you, Your Majesty, that we will never serve your gods or worship the gold statue you have set up.

Daniel 3:16–18

Not sure of the outcome, these three were ready to pay the ultimate price to be faithful to God.

Daniel's friends were commanded to worship a false god. In contrast, Daniel was prohibited by the government from worshiping the one true God. By continuing his practice of publicly praying three times a day, Daniel's civil disobedience earned him a trip to the lion's den (Daniel 6:1–28).

In both cases, government policy mattered. History shows that such policies are enormously consequential. Since America's laws, regulations, and presidential proclamations are sometimes antithetical to the Bible, we, too, must be prepared to enter the modern-day equivalents of a fiery furnace and a lion's den. In both situations, God miraculously intervened to save the righteous. But the Bible also gives accounts of righteous people who died for what was good and right in God's eyes: Abel, Naboth, Isaiah, John the Baptist, Jesus, and Stephen come to mind.

Today, God will choose to miraculously deliver some Christians and ordain equally devout Christians to sacrifice their lives. Either way, we must courageously sacrifice everything to follow God. We must heed Peter, Jesus, and Paul's warnings and exhortations that sacrifice and suffering will be part of the Christian life.

Fit for Service

To be fit for service, we must not be deceived. We must understand that the advancing totalitarian beast system comes with a smile, but will ultimately turn against every Jew and Christian in every nation, including America (Daniel 7:19–25; Revelation 12:17–13:10).

We must also remember Jesus' command to "Deny yourself, pick up your cross, and follow Me" (Luke 9:23). In America, this statement has made minimal difference. Perhaps somewhere, if forced to do so, someone might choose to do what Jesus said. However, receiving His command as optional was not Jesus' intent. Jesus was conveying something meant to be life-changing. We will either resist Jesus' call or we will give our lives to Him and for Him without reservation. Which will we choose? No one—including God—can make that decision for you. Will you be fit for service?

・・・

God has enlisted us for kingdom service for such a time as this. To be fit for service, we must seek Him wholeheartedly (Chapter 7), stand firm (Chapter 8), and suffer with Him and for Him (Chapter 9). But becoming fit for service is only a prerequisite to contend for the faith. It is to contending for the faith that we must turn our attention to next.

PART 3
Called to Contend

FIGHTING THE GOOD FIGHT 10

I have fought the good fight, I have finished the race, and I have remained faithful.

2 Timothy 4:7

Fighting, finishing, and faithful. Written near the end of Paul's life, these are the words of a contender. Words we would do well to follow today.

As we purpose to "fight the good fight," let's review the necessary groundwork to equip us to take action. In Section One, we explored America's troubling trajectory, the spiritual nature of the battle we are facing, God's view of nations, how God weighs nations, and America's status before God. This section concluded by showing that God is our primary threat because He is the One who sends corrective and final judgments to a nation. Indeed, like ancient Israel, America is in conflict with God.

In Section Two, we considered the necessary qualities to become fit for service. As those God has called to contend, we must have a seeking God lifestyle, stand firm against evil, and be willing to suffer with and for Jesus.

As we begin this section, *Called to Contend*, we consider the specific battlefronts we will engage in and what to do.

Battlefronts

The Church-Society-Government Paradigm is a helpful assessment tool. These are the three spheres God assesses to decide a nation's future. Therefore, naturally, these three areas are also the most important battlefronts between good and evil.

Once again, we must consider these questions. However, this time, not as assessment questions but as our three battlefronts:

- What is the church saying and doing?
- What does society want?
- Where is the government–federal, state, and local–leading us?

Each battlefront is critical, but they are not equal. The church must be our primary focus if we are to have any hope of influencing society and its leaders. With this in mind, let's look at "fighting the good fight" both as individuals and as the body of Christ.

It Begins With Us

But you, Timothy, are a man of God; so run from all these evil things. Pursue righteousness … Fight the good fight.

1 Timothy 6:11–12

Paul urged Timothy to commence fighting the good fight by running from evil and pursuing righteousness. This *running-from* and *running-to* approach to the Christian life is essential. If evil has infiltrated our lives, we have already lost. In contrast, righteousness

will strengthen us from within to engage the battle. Believers who are serious about contending for the faith must ponder:
1. Am I fleeing every form of evil?
2. Am I pursuing righteousness?

This is not to say that we need to achieve perfection before we contend for the faith, but it does mean we are making every effort to become Christ-like. With a *running-from* and *running-to* approach to the Christian life, we are fighting the good fight within and are ready to influence those around us.

Contending for the Church

A compromised church has already sabotaged its ability to influence culture. Author and international minister Art Katz (1929–2007) assessed the church, stating:

> The fact that the world can so easily tolerate us, the fact of the almost complete absence of reproach, let alone of persecution, is itself a shameful testimony that we are so like the world that we cannot be distinguished from it. We have lost even the difference—the sense of the difference—between that which is sacred and that which is profane. I believe that God could lay at the doorstep of the church the full responsibility for the present condition of the world.[1]

Although Katz gave the church this piercing evaluation, the body of Christ remains the most strategic entity on the planet.

Jude Contends

Jude's initial intention was to write to his brothers and sisters in Christ about their mutually shared treasure found in salvation. But because of recent developments, he found it to be a higher priority to urge them to contend for the purity of the faith within their fellowship:

> Dear friends, although I was very eager to write to you about the salvation we share, *I felt compelled to write and urge you to contend for the faith.* For certain individuals ... have secretly slipped in among you. They are ungodly people, who pervert the grace of our God into a license for immorality.

Jude 3–4 NIV (emphasis added)

Jude did not address evil outside the church—of which there would have been plenty—but addressed destructive beliefs taking hold within the church.

What was the issue? Jude called his friends to confront the erroneous idea that Christians can do whatever they feel like because God's grace will cover it.[2] Deceived by false teachers who had "slipped in," the church was on the precipice of dismissing holiness by neglecting the *run-from, run-to* approach to the Christian life.

Other New Testament writers highlight both saving grace *and* sanctifying grace. Grace is God's undeserved gift and unmerited favor at the moment of the new birth, and it is also God's empowering presence that propels Christians into greater godliness. Paul explains:

> For the grace of God has appeared that offers salvation to all people. It teaches us to say "No" to ungodliness and worldly passions, and to live self-controlled, upright and godly lives in this present age, while we wait for the blessed hope—the appearing of the glory of our great God and Savior, Jesus Christ, who gave himself for us to redeem us from all wickedness and to purify for himself a people

that are his very own, eager to do what is good. These, then, are the things you should teach. Encourage and rebuke with all authority.

Titus 2:11–15 NIV

God's grace should not make us feel comfortable with sin. Grace should empower us to live godly lives, purify us, and make us "eager to do what is good."

Similar to Jude, Paul called Titus to contend for the faith in his local fellowship. Once the radiance, power, and presence of the resurrected Christ have captured our gatherings, we will have something to offer our communities—our second battlefront.

Contending for Society

In 2022, I connected with a number of Christian and non-Christian activists through an organization called *We the Parents*. I soon volunteered to canvass neighborhoods to garner signatures to have corrupt school board members removed.

Why would I do such a thing? Years prior, we homeschooled our kids through high school and that chapter of our lives was long over. Even so, due to understanding the Bible and the outrageous wickedness promoted in our local public schools, I was deeply troubled that the youth in my community were being brainwashed.

We the Parents was forced to apply legal pressure on the school district through the Freedom of Information Act to obtain the teacher's training curriculum. The fact that the school district was trying to conceal these documents was in itself troubling. Once the training topics were disclosed, *We the Parents* discovered the workshops were largely comprised of LGBTQ advocacy and Marxist critical race theory ideology.

At the same time, media outlets denied that LGBTQ and Marxism were being promoted in the schools. They accused those who were trying to expose what was taking place as believing in outlandish conspiracy theories. However, as I talked to those employed in the school district, I gathered further evidence that it was not a lie nor a baseless conspiracy theory. Just as the training curriculum revealed, LGBTQ advocacy alongside critical race theory was taking place in my own community.

I was reminded that Jesus taught His followers to be "the salt of the earth," meaning it is the responsibility of Christians to preserve God's values in culture. The book of Proverbs also spoke to the situation:

Rescue those who are unjustly sentenced to die;
save them as they stagger to their death.
Don't excuse yourself by saying, "Look, we didn't know."
For God understands all hearts, and he sees you.
He who guards your soul knows you knew.
He will repay all people as their actions deserve.

Proverbs 24:11–12

God's Word, as well as the scientific data regarding LGBTQ lifestyles and the evil hidden within critical race theory, made it clear that local schools were promoting ideologies that would lead children and youth to "stagger to their death." This is not merely metaphorical or spiritual death—surely bad enough—but actual physical death.

People who undergo hormone therapy and transgender reassignment surgeries become suicidal at much higher rates than the general population. The Williams Institute at the University of California—Los Angeles reports that 81% of transgender adults in the U.S. have thought about suicide, 42% of transgender adults have attempted it, and 56% have engaged in non-suicidal self-injury over their lifetimes. The study concludes:

> While transgender and cisgender adults [that is, adults who identify according to their biological sex] reported similar rates of hazardous drinking and problematic drug use, transgender people were significantly more likely to experience poor mental health during their lifetimes. Compared to cisgender adults, transgender adults were seven times more likely to contemplate suicide, four times more likely to attempt it, and eight times more likely to engage in non-suicidal self-injury.[3]

Also heartbreaking are the online posts that describe the regret and despair of those who attempted to transition to the opposite sex. In a Reddit group comprised of 48,000 people who have de-transitioned—that is, transitioned to the opposite sex only to transition back to their biological sex—one member posted:

> I'm a 17 year old girl with a flat chest, a deep voice, a visible Adam's apple and some facial hair … I'm angry, I'm sad, I'm mad, I'm depressed, I'm hurt. I am grieving. I feel remorse. I can't deal with all this pain. I lost my breasts … I want a Time Machine so badly … I want my body back so badly.[4]

Reflecting on Proverbs 24:11–12, I knew that God wanted me to do something. If I failed to act, one day, I would answer to Him for my passivity. Could I truly claim I didn't know what was taking place in society in general and in my community specifically? Or could I tell God that I was aware but had accidently underestimated the importance of these issues?

Additional passages further clarified that confronting sin and contending for the faith is about loving people. Being the salt of the earth by publicly representing God's values is how we love our communities.

Contending for Government

Central to engaging the government sphere is electing those who are not anti-God, anti-Bible, and antiChrist. It also includes holding those who govern the people accountable to do what is good and right. Many Christians break out in a rash when the government is mentioned at church. *Here we go again with politics.* However, as demonstrated biblically and historically in Chapter Four, government is one of the three areas God assesses to decide a nation's future.

The kings of Israel were either commended for doing what was right in the sight of God or condemned for doing what was evil. Whether ancient kings or modern policymakers, what leaders choose has far-reaching implications. Ultimately, those who govern will either engender God's blessing or incite His judgment. Let us not entertain a false sense of security that the government is of no concern to God and that the church is exempt from influencing this sphere.

Paul highlights the need to intercede for this battlefront, connecting the choices of our political leaders with the fruitfulness of the gospel.

> I urge you, first of all, to pray for all people. Ask God to help them; intercede on their behalf, and give thanks for them. *Pray this way for kings and all who are in authority* so that we can live peaceful and quiet lives marked by godliness and dignity. This is good and pleases God our Savior, who wants everyone to be saved and to understand the truth.
>
> 1 Timothy 2:1–4 (emphasis added)

It is vital that we are informed about what is taking place in government at the local, state, and federal levels and intercede for our leaders.

Called to Contend

I trust your interest is piqued to contend for the faith in the church, society, and government. I only wish it was as simple as correcting heresy in our local fellowships, canvassing neighborhoods to influence school boards, and interceding for those who govern us. While each of these action steps are helpful, they will fall short in creating the systemic changes necessary to see God's purposes accomplished.

• • •

It is now time to take a deeper look at how to contend for faith in the church, society, and government spheres.

IN THE CHURCH 11

He [Jesus] is the one we proclaim, admonishing and teaching everyone with all wisdom, so that we may present everyone fully mature in Christ. To this end I strenuously contend with all the energy Christ so powerfully works in me.

Colossians 1:28–29 NIV (emphasis added)

Before we will influence entire communities, our local fellowships must be transformed into Christ-like, Spirit-empowered, biblically-rooted, faith-filled, wise, sacrificial, radiant expressions of the living God. To observe a lack of fruit, power, and holiness in the church while superficially stating, "God is in control" is an approach to church life that is not found in the Bible. What is found in God's Word? As Paul states above, strenuously contending with the energy of Christ that so powerfully works within us to see "everyone fully mature in Christ."

Highlighted in the previous chapter, Jude urged Christians to "contend for the faith" by confronting false teachers and their heresies. The writer of Hebrews brings another aspect of contending for the body of Christ into view:

Be careful then, dear brothers and sisters. Make sure that your own hearts are not evil and unbelieving, turning you away from the living God. You must warn each other every day, while it is still "today," so that none of you will be deceived by sin and hardened against God.

Hebrews 3:12–13

Warning each other about the deceptiveness of sin is central to contending for the life of the church. And when sin has taken root, we must diligently uproot and dispose of it through heartfelt repentance.

The First Century Church

Jesus began His ministry calling everyone to repent (Matthew 4:17; Mark 1:15). Jesus' last recorded words in the New Testament were exhortations for local churches to repent (Revelation 2:1–3:22). If Jesus' first and last words were to call people to repent from specific sins, perhaps our local fellowships need a fresh call to repent.

Jesus was not alone in calling the church to repent. Addressing his Christian "brothers and sisters" three times in his opening remarks, James implored his readers to "Get rid of all the filth and evil in your lives, and humbly accept the word God has planted in your hearts, for it has the power to save your souls" (James 1:21). Later, James urged these believers to repent again declaring: "Don't you realize that friendship with the world makes you an enemy of God?" James' point is clear. Repent and contend against worldliness, or you will find yourself contending against God. James continues, "Wash your hands, you sinners; purify your hearts, for your loyalty is divided between God and the world" (James 4:4–10). Strong words for the church in his day and often overlooked in churches today.

Paul also admonished the body of Christ to repent. He exhorted believers in Colossae to "get rid of anger, rage, malicious behavior, slander, and dirty language" and to start living with "tenderhearted mercy, kindness, humility, gentleness, and patience" (Colossians 3:8, 12; Also see Ephesians 4:22–24). Peter warned believers not to revert to pre-Christian lifestyles by exhorting the body of Christ: "Don't slip back into your old ways of living to satisfy your own desires. You didn't know any better then. But now you must be holy in everything you do, just as God who chose you is holy" (1 Peter 1:14–15a). John called Christians to a repentant lifestyle, stating, "If we claim we have no sin, we are only fooling ourselves and not living in the truth. But if we confess our sins to him, he is faithful and just to forgive us our sins and to cleanse us from all wickedness" (1 John 1:8–9).

Contending for the church begins with a clear call to repentance alongside a renewed surrender to Christ's lordship. If we choose to do so, this clean slate will not only engender God's favor and the activity of the Holy Spirit among us, the church will also become a potent force within our communities.

Jesus' Example

With eyes aflame with holy fire, Jesus appeared to John to affirm and warn the churches in Asia Minor. He called five of these local fellowships to turn from specific sins: lackluster love of God, sexual immorality, idolatry, hypocrisy, giving up, lethargy, lukewarmness, self-sufficiency, and materialism (Revelation 2:4, 14, 20; 3:1–2, 17). Jesus called these Christians to thoroughly change their lives by urging them to remember what their lives were like when they first loved God, to do the deeds they did when they had first come to faith, to live with an undivided faith, to hold fast to the truth, to pursue spiritual life, and open the church door to Jesus so they could truly know Him (Revelation 2:5, 14–16, 25; 3:2–3, 20).

Jesus also contended for the hearts of His people by promising breathtaking rewards for all who would repent. He guaranteed access to the tree of life in Paradise, positions of authority over the nations after His return, and hearing their names announced to the Father and the angels (Revelation 2:7, 26–27; 3:5).

Jesus also warned these churches of the devastating consequences if they chose not to repent. He promised to remove His lampstand, meaning He would personally close their church doors or at least be absent from their gatherings. According to Lifeway Research, in 2021, 3,000 Protestant churches opened, while more than 4,500 closed.[1] Further, Jesus warned that He would actively wage war against unrepentant churches. He would allow suffering. And He would spew lukewarm Christians out of His mouth (Revelation 2:5, 16, 22–23; 3:16). Sobering indeed.[2]

Living Water

Too often, we assume that identifying sin and calling upon people to repent will produce guilt. However, just the opposite is true—not identifying and repenting of sexual immorality, worldly loves, bitterness, and other besetting sins is what will make us miserable. Indeed, we will remain in bondage to everything God intended to free us.

Jesus taught that life with Him is best described as "rivers of living water flowing from one's innermost being" (John 7:38 NASB).

A personal experiential walk with Jesus for sure, but Paul also called Christians to experience Jesus' living water as a community when he called the Ephesian church to be "filled up to all the fullness of God" (Ephesians 3:14–19; 4:10–13). This was something that the Ephesian Christians were not yet experiencing, but Paul saw "filled to the fullness" as a wonderfully attainable corporate experience. Do we?

Contending Today

The East African Revival is a movement that was sparked in the late 19th century, advanced in waves throughout the 20th century,[3] and continues to see remarkable fruit in various locations today. These Africans learned to apply this powerful truth: the deeper the roots of repentance, the greater the fruits.

Through British missionaries and faith-filled indigenous Christians, the church grew dramatically from the 1880s to 1920. Yet, at the turn of the century, a "spiritual relapse" also characterized the church. After 1900, the movement continued to grow numerically but the presence and power of God gradually abated. Christians had become confused about their assurance of salvation while pagan practices, sexual immorality, and worldliness infiltrated the church.[4]

In the 1930s, Dr. J. E. Church, a British missionary, and ten indigenous leaders hosted numerous eight-day conferences to contend for the body of Christ. They addressed "sin, repentance, the new birth, separation [from the world by] 'Coming out of Egypt,' the Holy Spirit, and the victorious life." Not only through preaching but by spending considerable time simply reading Bible passages that addressed each of these topics, lives were dramatically changed.[5]

Prominent throughout the East African Revival were, "Confession of sin, restitution, apologies followed; many had dreams, sometimes receiving strong impressions to read certain verses of the Bible, which led them to put away some sin ... [Subsequently] preaching bands have gone out ... and very many are stirred."[6]

One eyewitness reported that there was no doubt of the Africans' "depth of their experience of Jesus Christ," which was accompanied by "tremendous joy." Also, their profound love for each other paved the way for a deeper fellowship "than one had ever dreamed of before." Koinonia (Greek for heartfelt fellowship) shifted from being a concept in the Bible to a glorious reality.[7]

Writing in the 1950s about the East African Revival, missionary Norman Grubb summarized that Christians learned to live with "the roof off and the walls down"—the roof off before God and the walls down before each other.[8] This transparent approach to the Christian life was central to continuous repentance and spiritual cleansing, spontaneous joy, life-changing koinonia, and the burden they carried for their "fellowmen and their Church."[9]

Wisconsin

When I was directing a campus ministry at the University of Wisconsin in 1995, God manifested His presence in our midst during a Christian gathering on a Friday evening in the Student Union. Two students from Wheaton College had come to share how public confession and repentance had changed their lives and how their campus was being transformed by the power and presence of Christ. As they concluded, God drew near, and students and campus ministers were suddenly in tearful brokenness over personal sin. God was dealing with us corporately, but His work was profoundly personal.

Before this meeting, I was confident that I had confessed unforgiveness and bitterness toward people who had wronged me over the years. However, during that special gathering of only 40–50 people, God showed me that I was living in denial. Deep down, I was still resentful toward people. Prior to this epiphany, I brushed off these wrongs as frustrating and disappointing, but I would not have connected them to anything that was impeding the "streams of living water" Jesus had promised. *We might not be filled to the fullness, but generally, I'm okay, and those around me are okay with God*, or so I thought.

During that divine encounter where everything was laid bare before me, I tasted a bit of what Isaiah experienced by being "undone" before God (Isaiah 6:1–6). In His palpable presence, my spirit became exceedingly vexed. Feeling compelled, I stood up before everyone and confessed in tears and brokenness deep-seated hatred, anger, and bitterness. After this public confession, I soon noticed "righteousness, peace, and joy in the Holy Spirit" manifesting in and through me (Romans 14:17). The streams of living water were once again a reality!

The book of Isaiah explains how brokenness over personal sin and repentance is a pathway to God's reviving presence:

> The high and lofty one who lives in eternity, the Holy One, says this: "I live in the high and holy place [but also] with those whose spirits are contrite and humble. I restore the crushed spirit of the humble and revive the courage of those with repentant hearts.
>
> Isaiah 57:15

At the UW, stagnant believers were transformed into spiritual dynamos. This season of God's holy presence and reviving work ushered in years of fruitfulness and influence throughout the campus.

Tennessee

In 2011, Candies Creek Baptist Church in Charleston, Tennessee saw a similar move of God. Night after night, revivalist Laine Johnson preached messages addressing spiritual apathy and waywardness within the church. Convicted of sin, once the first few people found freedom in Christ through public confession and repentance, others were stirred to turn from sin and experience similar freedom. This response was not limited to new believers—God exposed sin, transgressions, and iniquity within the hearts of longtime faithful church attendees and leaders who became broken over personal sin.

At Candies Creek, as God's life burst forth in numerous lives, the decision was made to extend the nightly services for four weeks. How do you get people to come to church for hours a day, not want to leave, and eagerly wait for the next meeting? When God manifests His presence, lives are changed, and nothing will keep His people away!

In East Africa, Wisconsin, and Tennessee, each fellowship contended for purity within the body of Christ. Each sought God in humility and took the rooting out of sin seriously. Each saw the radiance of Christ come back to their hearts, homes, and Christ's body. Contending for purity in the hearts of God's people must become one of our highest priorities today.

Even so, humility through repentance is not all that is needed to effectively contend for the spiritual vibrancy of the church. Church leadership must find its voice on cultural poison infiltrating the hearts and minds of God's people. If antiChrist mindsets go unchallenged, the body of Christ will compromise, descend into deception, and ultimately become useless. Jesus said, "What good is salt if it has lost its flavor? Can you make it salty again? It will be thrown out and trampled underfoot as worthless" (Matthew 5:13).

Finding Our Voice

To find our voice, we must assess what is taking place in culture through a biblical lens and expose spiritual lies and wickedness. We must not solely rely on news outlets, podcasts, and social media to inform our thinking. Within our local fellowships, Christians must hear a biblical response to the evil encroaching upon us and together determine the way forward.

Tragically, because church leadership rarely addresses what is taking place culturally, Christians who sit in church every week often have no idea what God's perspective is on the key issues of the day. Ironically, the church is not being censored or canceled by the culture—the church has censored itself. When silent on issues, we are violating what we are called to do: protect and build up each member of the body of Christ (Ezekiel 34:1–10; John 10:11–16; Ephesians 4:11–16).

As Jesus' return nears, the darkness will get darker with the gap between God's truth and cultural mindsets becoming greater and greater (Matthew 24:12; 2 Thessalonians 3:9–12; 2 Timothy 3:1–5). Let's identify a few cultural issues over which we must find our voice.

Perversion

Christians are bombarded and enticed by easy access to pornography, LGBTQ advocacy, and every sexual perversion imaginable through social media, movies, the Internet, and mainstream media. There are gray areas in the Bible, but human sexuality is not one of them. Paul exhorts the body of Christ:

God's will is for you to be holy, so stay away from all sexual sin. Then each of you will control his own body and live in holiness and honor—not in lustful passion like the pagans who do not know God and his ways. Never harm or cheat a fellow believer in this matter by violating his wife, for the Lord avenges all such sins, as we have solemnly warned you before.

1 Thessalonians 4:3–6

In 1996, Congress passed the Defense of Marriage Act (DOMA), which was signed into law by President Clinton. The purpose of DOMA was to legally define marriage as a union between one man and one woman. Same-sex marriages were not to be recognized as legally binding in any state because DOMA superseded state laws. As late as 2008, California passed Proposition 8, a state constitutional amendment to ban same-sex marriages.

But the definition of marriage soon changed. In 2015, the U.S. Supreme Court handed down a landmark decision, *Obergefell v. Hodges*, overturning all state and federal laws that prohibited same-sex marriage. Since this ruling, many legal ramifications for Christians have been either litigated in the courts or debated in legislatures:

- Can a Christian adoption agency deny the placement of children to same-sex couples?
- If Christian colleges and universities teach the biblical position on marriage, will these institutions be allowed to accept federal funding?
- Can churches, Christian ministries, and faith-based organizations deny leadership positions to people who are in same-sex unions?

- Can a Christian pastor be charged with a hate crime if he states that homosexual relationships are a sin?

The church must face the ramifications of the redefining of marriage. The reason that gay marriage and LGBTQ lifestyles are often embraced and sometimes advocated by Christians is because church leadership has yet to find its voice.

Exposing BLM

The church, the one institution with God's answer for racism, was curiously quiet after cities erupted in riots in the aftermath of George Floyd's death in 2020. As a result, deceived church members were sympathetic to Black Lives Matter, which played a key role in fomenting riots that destroyed local businesses, many of which were owned by ethnic minorities. It was vital to receive biblical instruction during this chaotic season, but churches typically remained silent. In contrast, African American scholar Voddie Baucham found his voice and contended for the body of Christ by explaining Black Lives Matter's war on Christianity:

> According to the Critical Social Justice (CSJ) view, the hegemonic power in the United States of America must include, but is not limited to, *all* of the following: white, male, heterosexual, cisgender, able-bodied, native-born, and Christian. That's right: Christianity is part of the oppressive hegemony. And according to some, it is the *most pernicious* aspect of it; it has and maintains "privilege," and contributes to oppression."[10]

Regarding BLM's cofounder, Patrisse Cullors, Baucham explains:

> In a now-viral video, Cullors identifies herself and her cofounders as "trained Marxists." Cullors is the protégé of Eric Mann, "former agitator of the Weather Underground domestic terror

organization." From him, she spent several years absorbing the Marxist-Leninist ideology that contributes significantly to her worldview. The organization's revolutionary Marxist origins and ethos are antithetical to the message of Christianity.[11]

Speaking to BLM's advocacy of sexual and gender perversion, Baucham continues:

> All three of BLM's founders are lesbians who were bothered by the fact that "Black liberation movements in this country have created room and space and leadership mostly for Black heterosexual, cisgender men, leaving women, who are often queer or transgender, either out of the movement or in the background to move the work forward with little or no recognition." They "recognized a need to center the leadership of women," particularly queer and transgender women.[12]

Sadly, Black Lives Matter, an anti-Christian, godless, Marxist, LGBTQ advocacy organization determined to divide and conquer America, was given the opportunity to promote great evil nationwide, while church members largely remained unaware of what was taking place from a biblical perspective.

Almost two years before Baucham published *Fault Lines* to awaken Christians to BLM's weaponizing of racism to undermine Christianity and destroy America, I was researching BLM's Marxist underpinnings and their spiritual practices. I did not discover the following from BLM critics but from BLM's own leadership.

In a UCLA-sponsored interview, Patrisse Cullors and BLM's Los Angeles director, Melina Abdullah, openly discussed contacting the spirits of the dead to inspire, strengthen, and direct them. Cullors remarked, "It's so important, not just for us to be in direct relationship with our people who have passed, but also for them to know that we've remembered them. I believe so many of them work through us."[13]

Abdullah shared how she laughs with Wakiesha, the spirit of a black woman found dead in a Los Angeles jail in 2016. Abdullah admits she was initially resistant to the spiritual aspect of her BLM training but later appreciated it as integral to their mission: "We become very intimate with the spirits we call on regularly. Each one seems to have a different presence and personality."[14] Cullors and Abdullah make this pagan practice sound wonderfully inspiring and ordinary, but it is forbidden by God (Deuteronomy 18:9–14).

When an organization is this antiChrist, this public, and this consequential to our churches and nation, we must ask why Christians and church leadership are silent. Why are we not contending for the mindsets of the faithful in the pews each week? Should we not expose BLM as a well-funded, Marxist, pagan movement? Should we not provide biblically-based racial reconciliation principles to replace BLM ideology? Or do we believe that Jesus does not want His followers to know His approach to healing racism in America?

The Right to Assemble

The COVID-19 pandemic highlighted many pressing threats, including the basic right for local congregations to choose to keep their doors open. In a radical departure from history and the U.S. Constitution, state governments, alongside local and state agencies, mandated churches to close their doors, labeling the church non-essential. In a distressing twist, marijuana shops, liquor stores, and strip clubs were deemed essential and allowed to stay open. Yet, many churches readily complied with government mandates to close their doors, even though these mandates defied our nation's belief in the separation of church and state.

Ironically, these decisions often revealed significant fear within the body of Christ. There was the fear of death, fear of the government, and fear that if church leadership chose to stay open, some members might disagree and leave the church. While claiming to be wise and measured, rarely has the church revealed itself to be so timid.

In many churches, elders decided to close the church doors "out of respect for the elderly." At the time, this decision sounded compassionate because people over 70 years old were at a much higher risk of dying of COVID-19 than younger people. However, why weren't churches kept open to let the elderly and others with health conditions make their own decision to self-quarantine? Whether hiding behind the elderly, fearing government reprisal, or making other excuses, churches chose to close their doors en masse.

Paradoxically, while churches closed, the U.S. and state Constitutions legally protected the right for churches to stay open and worship as they would choose. Just as Paul appealed to Roman law to aid him in his mission (Acts 22:22–29), so Christians in 2020 could have done the same. However, the fear narrative prevailed—even within the church—and the church once again followed the culture and, worse, stayed silent on what was good and right.

Pastor Jackie Hill provides a refreshing example of what it looks like to find one's voice. Hearing the alarming early reports and Dr. Fauci's advice to enforce "lockdowns for two weeks to slow the curve," Hill proposed keeping the church doors open. The elder board concluded that they could at least give people the option to meet and worship corporately if they so desired. Hill led the way in making this decision despite the fact Hill has a lung condition—the very organ the virus targets.

Hill and his leadership concluded that Scripture teaches that Christians are to assemble to worship and function as the body of Christ—something not possible when isolated at home watching services online (Hebrews 10:24–25). Also, reflecting upon the separation of church and state, the church affirmed that the government is not allowed to interfere with the decisions of a local assembly. The church's legal footing was secure.

As Hill sought the Lord, mindful of his own higher risk of death, Jesus' words kept coming to his mind, "The shepherd lays down his life for the sheep" (John 10:11). Hill and his elders chose to keep their church doors open to worship God together, encourage one another, and minister to each other.

As the months passed, Hill remained the only pastor in his denomination to stay open in the Minneapolis/St. Paul area. That is one church out of fifty-two that remained open. Standing alone, Hill contended for the flock God had charged him to oversee. Hill remained healthy, the church remained open, and attendance grew.[15]

False Teachers

Jesus, Jude, Peter, and Paul all warned of false teachers who either infiltrated the church in their day or would attempt to lead God's people astray before Jesus' return. Social media platforms are plentiful with those who are "declaring and decreeing" that God will save America, all the while neglecting to call God's people to humility and repentance.

While it sounds hopeful and exciting that "God is not done with America yet," these declarations are typically disconnected from God's Word. The Bible exhorts us to humble ourselves in fasting, prayer, and repentance, boldly speaking the truth, standing in righteousness, and sacrificing for the gospel. However, the "declare and decree" crowd has replaced God's Word with an easier way. Unfortunately, this easier way—declaring and decreeing that God will save America while the nation persists in hardened rebellion and celebration of sin—is not found in the Bible.

Pastor and Bible teacher Dr. Chuck Hetzler asks, "Where in the Bible, where in church history, has a great move of God ever been preceded by people simply declaring and decreeing?" His answer was, "Nowhere." What we do see in Scripture is the restoration of nations when God's people humble themselves, pray, seek God's face, and turn from their wicked ways (2 Chronicles 7:14).

Even more disturbing, some of these voices claim to be speaking the very words of God. God has strong words for those who speak from their own desires while claiming to speak for Him:

> "What sorrow awaits the false prophets who are following their own imaginations and have seen nothing at all!" O people of Israel, these prophets of yours are like jackals digging in the ruins. They have done nothing to repair the breaks in the walls around the nation. They have not helped it to stand firm in battle on the day of the Lord. Instead, they have told lies and made false predictions… Can your visions be anything but false if you claim, "This message is from the Lord," when I have not even spoken to you? Therefore, this is what the Sovereign Lord says: Because what you say is false and your visions are a lie, I will stand against you…I will raise my fist against all the prophets who see false visions and make lying predictions, and they will be banished from the community of

Israel…This will happen because these evil prophets deceive my people by saying, "All is peaceful" when there is no peace at all!

Ezekiel 13: 3–10

Since Scripture warns what happens to nations that continuously defy God, contending for the church includes warning others in the body of Christ of the danger America is facing. With false teachers and self-appointed "prophets" declaring that our best days are right around the corner, few of these "prophets" will warn the nation about anything. Therefore, it is even more important that those who are aware of our nation's dangerous trajectory warn the body of Christ of what is taking place.

Called to Contend

Jesus gave His life for the church. Contending for the body of Christ is worth our lives, too. God's radiance filling our hearts, homes, and churches starts with humble repentance. This includes humble confession before our brothers and sisters in Christ. Once these initial steps are taken, it is imperative to live with the roof off and the walls down.

We must also find our voice on every cultural issue that the Bible speaks to. The Bible is the certain Word of God. We must proclaim all of it within our local fellowships, not just the passages we prefer to highlight. Addressing sexual perversion, BLM, and other godless Marxist schemes, government overreach to close our church doors, and warning others of false teachers only begins to address what we are called to confront. The health of the church, the health of the sheep, depends upon addressing every issue the Bible speaks to.

∙ ∙ ∙

Although the most important battlefront, a Christian's call to contend is not limited to the church. God expects us to put on His armor and influence society—our families, friends, neighbors, workplace, and communities. We must now turn our attention to the second battlefront.

IN SOCIETY

You are the salt of the earth ...
You are the light of the world.

Matthew 5:13–14

From *Forerunners of America's* inception, God strongly impressed upon me how much more Christians will need to trust in Him and the Holy Spirit's power in the days ahead. Bill Bright (1921–2003), founder of Campus Crusade for Christ (renamed Cru in 2011), often taught, "The Christian life is not difficult. It is impossible. This is why we need the enabling of the Holy Spirit." Quoting Paul, Bright challenged Christians to continuously "be filled with the Spirit" (Ephesians 5:18).

Paul's instructions on the Holy Spirit include how to walk in the Spirit (Galatians 5:16-26), bear the fruit of the Spirit (Galatians 5:22–23), practice the gifts of the Spirit (1 Corinthians 12:4–11), and live in the "goodness and peace and joy in the Holy Spirit" (Romans 14:17). In every generation, understanding the person and work of the Holy Spirit is foundational. But in light of today's encroaching evil, the battle of the ages, imminent corrective and final judgments, and unique pressures that precede Jesus' return, walking in the power of the Spirit is vital.

Returning to Our Roots

The book of Acts documents God's Word going out in the power of the Holy Spirit despite persecution at almost every turn. During Paul's second missionary journey, the enemies of the gospel cried out in despair, "These men who have turned the world upside down have come here also" (Acts 17:6 ESV).

Through the anointed proclamation of the gospel, healings, resurrections, demonic deliverances, and outpourings of the Holy Spirit, thousands of people became followers of Jesus Christ, and culture itself was often changed. One such societal transformation took place 60 miles north of Jerusalem:

> A great wave of persecution began that day [the day of Stephen's martyrdom], sweeping over the church in Jerusalem; and all the believers except the apostles were scattered through the regions of Judea and Samaria ... But the believers who were scattered preached the Good News about Jesus wherever they went. Philip, for example, went to the city of Samaria and told the people there about the Messiah. Crowds listened intently to Philip because they were eager to hear his message and see the miraculous signs he did. Many evil spirits were cast out, screaming as they left their victims. And many who had been paralyzed or lame were healed. So there was great joy in that city.
>
> Acts 8:1–8

Such remarkable acts of God should not be viewed as an aberration from what God desires today. Instead, like the people of Samaria, we should pursue and celebrate with "great joy" those coming to faith, physically healed, and delivered from demonic influence. Such phenomena are sometimes foreign to Western Christians, yet God's miraculous works are often witnessed today in Central America, South America, Africa, Asia, and the Middle East.

In America, we need to be reminded that Scripture not only teaches us about the God of the Bible but *the supernatural God of the Bible*. The writer of Hebrews explains that Jesus is unchanging (Hebrews 13:8); thus, God is able to move through us and transform communities, just as He did during the first-century.

Will we follow God into such fruitful ministry? Will we look at what is recorded in Scripture not as exceptions, but as examples to follow? In this spirit, with an eye to influencing society, let's briefly look at the lives of Stephen and Philip.

Mind and Spirit

Prior to Philip's ministry in Samaria (Acts 8:1–40), Philip, Stephen, and five others were chosen to remedy a racist situation: the Hebraic widows were being favored over the Greek-speaking Jewish widows in the distribution of food. To resolve this situation, the apostles looked for Christians who were "well respected and full of the Spirit and wisdom" (Acts 6:3). Those selected would have been respected due to their Godly character, but how were the qualifications of fullness of the Spirit and wisdom apparent to others?

Stephen was known as a man "full of God's grace and power" who performed many miracles. Regarding wisdom, his adversaries were unable to keep up with him in a debate (Acts 6:8–10). Similarly, God used Philip to move the crowds through a reasonable, thoughtful, persuasive gospel message and through the unexplainable (Acts 8:4–13). Both Philip and Stephen's ministries were characterized by *the life of the mind* (wisdom) and *life in the Spirit* (phenomena that could only be explained by God moving in their midst). Employing the practical aspects of this paradigm—*the life of the mind and life in the Spirit*—is foundational to influencing society.

The Good News of the Kingdom

Further, Philip proclaimed a message centered on "the Good News of the kingdom of God and name of Jesus Christ" (Acts 8:12). We are familiar with the name of Jesus Christ, but are we preaching the Good News of the kingdom of God? What is the Good News of the kingdom?

Every kingdom has a king. Philip knew that the Samaritans needed to hear that a new King had arrived: Jesus the Messiah, the anointed One, the Son of God. Culturally, the Samaritans understood that transferring kingdoms entailed forsaking the current king to give one's full allegiance to the new king. Therefore, the Samaritans would also have understood that Philip was calling them to follow Jesus as their king—the King of glory—and, therefore, fully transfer their allegiance to Him.

Once a community crowns Jesus as King, and thus comes under His rule and reign, everything good takes place. This includes experiencing forgiveness of sins, vanquishing wickedness, miracles, and shalom (God's peace) permeating society. The truth of the Good News of the kingdom was not only explained by Philip, but as people responded they began to experience these kingdom realities. The arrival of King Jesus and His kingdom was good news indeed!

Further, Jesus taught us to pray that God's kingdom will come to earth—that is into our communities—and that His will be done right here, right now as it is in heaven (Matthew 6:9–10). When praying the Lord's Prayer, we are literally praying for God's rule and reign to increasingly influence our own lives and expand throughout our communities.

Advancing God's Kingdom
Further, Jesus, Philip, and Paul modeled the three primary ways God's kingdom advances to change society: Preaching the Good News, delivering people from demonic influence, and physical healings. We must not think of these three kingdom activities as separate ministry modes to employ according to one's preference or comfort level. We should view these activities as simultaneous realities that clear the way for God's rule and reign to expand on earth. Indeed, God is about the business of replacing the kingdom of darkness with the kingdom of His beloved Son—and it will take all three ministry modes to do so.

These aspects of expanding God's kingdom on earth were central to Jesus' training of His disciples. Luke records that Jesus gave his disciples "power and authority to cast out all demons and to heal all diseases," and told them to "tell everyone about the Kingdom of God" (Luke 9:1–2). Describing the disciples' ministry, Luke continues, "So they began their circuit of the villages, preaching the Good News and healing the sick" (Luke 9:6). Matthew also recounts Jesus' instructions to His disciples:

> Go and announce to them that the Kingdom of Heaven is near [preaching]. Heal the sick, raise the dead, cure those with leprosy, and cast out demons [healing and deliverance]. Give as freely as you have received!
>
> Matthew 10:7–8

Jesus' goal was to see His disciples duplicate His ministry. And He intended this powerful *life of the mind and life in the Spirit* ministry to be passed down throughout the centuries, including to us today. We know this not only because Christians throughout the book of Acts ministered in these ways but also because Jesus told His disciples:

> I have been given all authority in heaven and on earth. Therefore, go and make disciples of all the nations, baptizing them in the name of the Father and the Son and the Holy Spirit. Teach these new disciples to obey all the commands I have given you. And be sure of this: I am with you always, even to the end of the age.
>
> Matthew 28:18–20

If these "new disciples" throughout the last 2,000 years were being taught "to obey all the commands" Jesus gave His initial disciples, this includes Jesus' commands to preach the Good news of the Kingdom of God, heal the sick, and deliver people from demonic influence. Since He is with us "even to the end of this age," we must trust Him to do these works through us. This, too, will be vital in influencing our communities.

My Story

When I came to Christ, God showed me the importance of reading, studying, and teaching His Word, as well as sharing the gospel. These activities were, and still are, a joy. There is power in the Word! However, the first time I dealt with the demonic, God almost cornered me, practically making me do it.

It was the fall of 2002 and I was speaking to more than a hundred college students at a weekend Christian retreat. My messages had nothing to do with proclaiming God's kingdom, healing, or demonic deliverance. My message centered on calling these students to freedom in Christ through humbly repenting of specific sins.

After the message and near the end of the response time, Katherine, a sophomore, made her way to the front of the room to confess her waywardness. Her confession was unlike any I had heard before: "Sometimes you hear voices in your head, and you know that they are not your own." Suddenly, what appeared to be involuntary, her head snapped away from the microphone. Struggling to turn her head toward the audience, she tried again, "Sometimes you hear..." her head snapped again. Again, she tried. Again, her head snapped.

I sensed the crowd waiting for me to do something. But what? I had no background, teaching, or training in the spiritual battle raging just a few feet away. Rattled, I prayed, "God, what should I do?" Suddenly, I felt compelled to stand up and step onto the platform. My fear vanished, and I looked directly into her eyes. To my surprise, before I said anything, she screamed and threw herself to the floor.

Sound like victory? An exciting way to spend a Saturday evening? Honestly, I gulped and thought, *what in the world do I do now?* The only thought that came to me—thankfully it came quickly—was to command the enemy to leave. I said, "In the name of Jesus, come out!" At that moment, God moved mightily, and Katherine was set free.

Later, a few of us ministered to Katherine privately. God answered our prayers, showing us each step to take, each question to ask, each Scripture to read, and each prayer to pray to solidify her newfound freedom in Christ.

As the evening unfolded, a number of students came to faith in Jesus as their Savior and Lord. They had witnessed the reality of the spirit realm, as well as the power of God and eagerly committed their lives to Christ. And, like Samaria, there was much joy!

Societal Impact

Society is first and foremost transformed by people coming to faith. For those who were born again that weekend, they had a new story to tell. A story of encountering God, believing in Christ, finding forgiveness and cleansing, and seeing someone set free of the evil one's power.

When these students returned home, they did not keep their encounter with the living God to themselves. Friends, family, classmates, and coworkers heard their account of God's presence and power—and their own changed lives. This is how societal transformation begins: the Word of God going out in power with the works of God changing lives.

Cornered Again

God did something similar to get my attention regarding His ability to heal people. In 2010, I was giving a seminar to ministry leaders at Montana State University. Inspired by Katherine's changed life and others since that special weekend, I chose to teach about how to see God's kingdom expand. Further, Paul's declaration, "The kingdom of God is not about words, but about power," was something I was coming to understand more and more (1 Corinthians 4:20).

The daylong seminar was moving along, but most of those in attendance seemed more interested in lunch than seeing God's kingdom advance. When we broke for lunch, I found a seat next to a large, bearded campus minister named Taylor and three others. Not only did Taylor look the part of a Montanian, but he had also spent extensive time in Alaska doing whatever large, bearded men do in Alaska.

Sitting down, I asked Taylor how he was doing, expecting the usual "good" response. Instead, he replied, "I have this shoulder pain that's been going on for months, and it's really a problem. Nothing is helping." I felt that nudge in my spirit to do something, but inwardly groaned and thought, *Lord, You have got to be kidding. I'm tired from teaching and facilitating for three hours. I don't have the faith for this right now.* Also, Taylor did not mention his shoulder pain to receive prayer. I thought, *he's not looking for prayer and I don't want to pray,* and began to eat my lunch.

Nevertheless, God's Spirit started to press on my spirit about the pertinence of what I had taught all morning. With this inner turmoil growing, I thought, *why am I not doing something?* Reluctantly, I turned to Taylor and said, "In light of everything we looked at this morning in the Bible, can I pray for your shoulder?" He agreed.

I finished praying and returned to my lunch. Nothing appeared to happen and I was happy to move on. But again, I felt the Lord disturbing my spirit. This time He was bothering me because none of us at the table had checked with Taylor to see if he was healed. Not sure where this was going, I turned to him and asked if he had felt anything when we prayed.

"No," he replied.

I asked, "Can you lift your arm? Show us your range of motion? Do you have any pain?"

Quite uninspired, Taylor shrugged but began to lift his arm and move it around. Suddenly, he looked at me with an intensely furrowed brow—what I perceived to be anger. I feared I had done something wrong, and his shoulder felt worse. Taylor shouted, "HOLY C@#%!!!!"

His outburst shook me, but I shouted back, "WHAT HAPPENED?"

He responded, "All of the pain is completely gone!"

Those at our table looked at each other in amazement.

Shortly, I asked Taylor to share his experience with the whole group, and he agreed. But rather than explaining what happened to his shoulder, Taylor started sharing something else:

> I want to confess and apologize to Marshall [another minister]. He has often talked about God doing miracles and I dismissed him and his "faith-talk" as ridiculous. Marshall, I am sorry. A few minutes ago, I received prayer for my shoulder pain, and now I am completely healed.

Not only was Taylor's shoulder restored, but through his confession, God also healed his relationship with a Christian brother.

Six months later, I was back in Montana, ministering to the same ministries on repentance, forgiveness, and freedom in Christ. I saw Taylor and asked him about his shoulder. Grinning from ear to ear, he said it had remained 100 percent healed. A few months later, I saw him again, and laughing, he said, "You don't need to ask! I have no shoulder pain."

Until that seminar at Montana State, I had had a lot of experience sharing the gospel and teaching the Bible but had not fully embraced God's kingdom ministry; that is, the gospel of the kingdom going out in power, demonic deliverance, and physical healings. Since my experiences with Katherine and Taylor, this type of ministry has become a regular part of my Christian life. The Word of God and the miraculous works of God—*the life of the mind and life in the Spirit*—is where contending for society often starts.

Broader Scope

In his book, *The Kingdom Is Yours*, renowned Presbyterian pastor and international minister Louis Evans (1897–1981) addresses Christ's mandate to see His kingdom expand throughout the world:

Christ came to earth for a specific reason; to bring this world and humanity back to fellowship with God again. The world, this celestial ball, has rolled out of the garden of God's will. Christ came to bring it back and place it in the hand of God, and this is your holy task and mine—to help Him do just that ... to bring this world and civilization back to God. This is our royal partnership with Christ, this is the vital meaning of living. Without this we have merely existed, we have never lived... Many of us breathe physically, but we are not alive spiritually to this great purpose of our day.[1]

Influencing society with the redemptive work of Christ in the power of the Holy Spirit is where we will all become truly alive.

Jesus' Mandate

In the midst of showing His followers what a Word-centered, Spirit-empowered, kingdom-expanding ministry looks like, Jesus gave His followers a mandate. A mandate that will help prepare more people to hear the gospel. A mandate that will see our Father receive far more glory throughout all of society. A mandate that will hold back spiritual darkness from dominating our communities.

In the Sermon on the Mount, Jesus explains that anyone who becomes a citizen of His kingdom will become part of His global mission to influence every facet of society. According to Jesus, this will happen when each Christian does his or her part as "the salt of the earth" and "light of the world" (Matthew 5:13–16).

With Jesus identifying our scope as "the earth" and "the world," we are to be Jesus' representatives, quite literally, everywhere. In other words, every person in every country is to be influenced by God's people, God's presence, and God's principles. In another teaching, Jesus adds,

"The kingdom of heaven is like yeast that a woman took and mixed into about sixty pounds of flour until it worked all through the dough" (Matthew 13:33). The body of Christ must influence every family, social network, business, profession, neighborhood, government agency, medical facility, and school throughout each of our communities. This is what God's kingdom kneaded throughout the dough will look like.

Salty Living

Salt adds flavor. It makes people thirsty. It was once used as a preservative in meat. We, too, should add the flavor of God's goodness, presence, and power in our spheres of influence to see people become thirsty for more—all the while preserving God's values.

This does not mean we are always reading Bible verses to our coworkers, at school board meetings, or even at home. It does mean we are living God's truth and that we speak His truth as we have opportunities to do so. For instance, at work, we may be tempted to compromise our integrity by cutting corners that customers will never know about. However, honesty is important to God—He sees and cares about how we represent Him. Christians must choose to have integrity at work in every situation and help coworkers do likewise. In doing so, we are being salty on the job.

To be the salt of the earth, we are also to speak the truth to expose cultural lies. How will we respond if a friend tells us that their child is pursuing a transgender lifestyle? We can tell the truth that transitioning rarely brings about the results that the person is hoping to see. We can read Bible passages that explain that God created humanity, and He biologically assigns each person his or her gender. Or we may point to the scientific impossibility of changing gender. Or we may point them to the heartbreaking stories online of individuals suffering due to hormone therapy and sex-reassignment surgery. When we encourage people to embrace their biological sex, we are being the "salt of the earth" because we are advocating God's design.

God has something to say about everything taking place in culture. How could He not? He presides over civilization, created each person, and knows how people function best. Everything is laid bare before His eyes and He calls us to be His ambassadors with the gospel first, and to everything else taking place in culture second. This "everything else" is often overlooked. And it is this topic we need to address next.

A Remarkable Example

Some Bible scholars believe that the four beasts in Daniel 7 do not represent four empires leading up to Jesus' *first* coming, but describe four empires leading up to Jesus' *second* coming. Following this interpretation, the first beast described in Daniel 7, which looks like a lion, is interpreted as the British Empire—the greatest empire by land mass in history.[2] Notably, this beast has the wings of an eagle that are plucked off. Some scholars believe that this is a reference to the American colonies securing their independence from Great Britain at the conclusion of the Revolutionary War in 1783.

Daniel states, "As I watched, its wings were pulled off, and it was left standing with its two hind feet on the ground, like a human being. And it was given a human mind" (Daniel 7:4). Remarkably, about the time the American colonies declared their independence, the British Empire underwent a series of changes that resulted in a moral transformation of the Empire. British society changed from being beastly, like a ferocious lion, to that of a person standing on two feet with a reasonable mind.

Whether the British Empire's transformation is the fulfillment of Daniel's vision, we can decide later. For now, let's look at what God did to society through the hands and hearts of His faithful followers.

British Depravity

Lawlessness is emboldened when a society is not held responsible for its evils. The British Empire was no exception. In his book *Amazing Grace*, Eric Metaxas explains,

> Entirely surprising to most of us, life in eighteenth-century Britain was particularly brutal, decadent, violent, and vulgar ... All of the social problems that would plague eighteenth-century Britain had come to full flower, having been unchecked by the social conscience of genuine Christian faith for nearly two hundred years. The unfortunate effects of religion's retreat were everywhere.[3]

In addition to the ongoing evil of the slave trade, alcoholism was rampant throughout all of Britain, even on display during sessions of Parliament. The king's sons were known as wildly promiscuous, as was much of the culture. The hopelessness and misery of the poor were visible everywhere. Public hangings for petty crimes and the public burning of the corpses were common and often viewed as entertainment.

In London, 25 percent of all unmarried women were prostitutes, with many employed at brothels to support their gin habit. Child prostitution (pedophilia) and oppressive child labor were widespread. Public cruelty to animals was an additional twisted form of entertainment, feeding the elites' assessment of the lower classes as brutish.[4]

Salt and Light on the Way

William Wilberforce (1759–1833), a member of Parliament and close friend to the Prime Minister, became a Christian in 1785 at the age of 26. His life quickly became so unrecognizable in desires, thoughts, values, and activities that he referred to his conversion the rest of his life as "the Great Change."[5]

Wilberforce's constant ministry to others and numerous responsibilities in Parliament kept him exceedingly busy, yet he sought God three hours a day. Records reveal that he and his closest friends' schedules revolved around Bible reading and prayer—or, as Paul put it, "seeking things above" (Colossians 3:1)—from 5:00-6:00 a.m., 12:00-1:00 p.m., and 5:00-6:00 p.m.[6] In light of God's call on His life, Wilberforce recognized the need to seek God continuously and rely on His intervention constantly.

Goodness Matters

Wilberforce is famous for being used by God to abolish slavery throughout the British Empire. However, freeing the slaves was only one of many changes that took place throughout society under Wilberforce's overarching goal to see "goodness become fashionable" again.[7]

Wilberforce understood how God's goodness intersects culture. Paul explains, "In the past he [God] permitted all the nations to go their own ways, but he never left them without evidence of himself and his goodness. For instance, he sends you rain and good crops and gives you food and joyful hearts" (Acts 14:16–17). To Wilberforce, if God is good to all, Christians should be good to all (Matthew 5:43–45). This understanding is vital to effectively contend for the faith in society.

The benefits humanity receives from God's goodness are everywhere. Yet, Jesus stated that people would also receive His goodness directly through Christians: "Let your good deeds shine out for all to see, so that everyone will praise your heavenly Father" (Matthew 5:16). When we do good deeds, those around us may not turn to faith in Christ immediately but God is using our good deeds to point people toward the Source of goodness—a goodness that transcends this world.

Wilberforce also believed that every person is created in God's image and should be treated as sacred. One must love one's neighbor as oneself, whether that neighbor is a Christian or not, and we must, as Jesus said, do to others as we would have them do to us.[8] All of this is central to influencing those around us.

Wilberforce's Calling

Wilberforce wrote, "God almighty has set before me two great objects: the suppression of the slave trade and the reformation of manners."[9] His work to stop the slave trade altered the course of civilization. But what about his other calling to reform manners? What was this ambition, and was he successful?

To Wilberforce, teaching people to say "please" and "thank you" and have better table manners was, at most, a small part of what he meant by the reformation of manners. However, if we recognize his goal as transforming society through moral principles to help people and restrain evil, we would be much closer to what he meant. Metaxas explains:

> By "manners" he did not mean anything having to do with etiquette but rather what we would call "habits" or "attitudes"; there was also a distinctly moral aspect to his use of the phrase, though not in the puritanical sense. He wished to bring civility and self-respect into a society that long since had spiraled down into vice and misery.[10]

The Sermon on the Mount was given early in Jesus' ministry and given to those who had not yet come to faith in Christ (Matthew 5:1, 7:28). In addition to explaining what it looks like to walk with God,

Jesus told his listeners how to live moral lives (Matthew 5:32, 37, 39, 42, 6:2, 19–21, 7:1–5). Like Jesus, Wilberforce—throughout his reformation of manners—was pointing people to a life honorable to God, which would bring civility to society and prepare them to come to faith later.

Luke records that people who embrace "noble character" are more likely to come to faith in Jesus:

> As soon as it was night, the believers sent Paul and Silas away to Berea. On arriving there, they went to the Jewish synagogue. Now the Berean Jews were of more noble character than those in Thessalonica, for they received the message with great eagerness and examined the Scriptures every day to see if what Paul said was true. As a result, many of them believed, as did also a number of prominent Greek women and many Greek men.
>
> Acts 17:10–12 NIV

It was bringing a sense of right and wrong; that is, some sense of an active conscience, a desire for goodness, and some desire for more noble character that Wilberforce actively promoted throughout British culture.

Heart Transformation?

As a prominent figure in government, Wilberforce understood that passing laws to promote goodness throughout society would not transform the human heart. A transformed heart is only realized through a genuine encounter with Christ—what Paul referred to as becoming "a new creation" (2 Corinthians 5:17).

Nevertheless, Wilberforce advocated changing cultural mindsets through legislation by punishing lesser crimes to see people deterred from committing greater crimes. He wrote to a friend, "We should at least so far remove the obtrusiveness of temptation, that it may not provoke the appetite, which might otherwise be dormant and inactive."[11]

Wilberforce was motivated to protect society from itself through the advancement of righteous public policy, and the results were astonishing. He brought "a concern for the poor and a social conscience into society at large" such that these attitudes and habits became "culturally mainstream."[12] Metaxas summarizes,

> It's not too much to say that this single observation [the need to punish lesser crimes to give society a conscience before committing greater crimes] was the lever by which little Wilberforce replaced an entire world of brutality and misery with another of civility and hope, one that we now refer to as the Victorian era.[13]

To further salt the earth, Wilberforce started Proclamation Societies. Using the King's own proclamation, which urged citizens to live with decency, these societies soon proliferated throughout Britain. God used them to change cultural expectations among Christians, nominal Christians, and the irreligious alike.[14] Embracing this "salt of the earth" approach, God used Wilberforce and his friends to stop, and even reverse, cultural decay, as well as point people to the Giver of all goodness.

Proclaiming Christ

Wilberforce and his Christian friends were known as the Clapham Sect (a.k.a. Clapham Circle, Clapham Group, Clapham Saints). They did not view their Christian calling as a choice between social reform or preaching the gospel. Helping the poor, changing cultural mindsets, and stopping slavery was not a replacement for leading as many people as possible to faith in Christ. The one (the reformation of manners) was to help the other (see more people come to faith), and both were to glorify God.

His personal conversations and journal entries reveal that Wilberforce was an unstoppable evangelist. Wherever he went, he tried "to bring the question around to eternity," even writing notes about each person and how to best turn conversations to the gospel. He called these topics "launchers" and used them with everyone he could.[15]

A Prophet?
Similar to an Old Testament prophet, Wilberforce spoke boldly about Britain's departure from God. He was concerned that what was parading around as Christianity was not Christianity at all. While there were numerous manifestations of this problem—much like America today—he was particularly troubled by the feeble version of Christianity modeled by the clergy.

To address that the emperor (clergy) had no clothes, on April 12, 1797, Wilberforce published a book, *A Practical View of the Prevailing Religious System of Professed Christians, in the Higher and Middle Classes of this Country, Contrasted with Real Christianity*.[16] His book went through several printings and was influential among the upper class, as well as the general population. Metaxas explains the strategic nature of this book:

> Real Christianity had evaporated from England principally because it was woven into the social fabric and therefore was easier to ignore and take for granted. "Christianity especially," he wrote, "has always thrived under persecution. For then it has no lukewarm professors." Wilberforce was exactly right. Not only was there no persecution of Christianity in England at that time, but the entire nation was officially Christian—in name only. England's pulpits were filled

with just such "lukewarm professors" lukewarmly professing a lukewarm faith that thrilled no one and challenged no one ... In his book Wilberforce was essentially calling Britain to repent, to turn back to the true faith.[17]

Societal transformation will always include God's "now" message on every cultural issue, but often this message needs to have a laser focus on the church itself. This was certainly true in eighteenth-century Britain.

Clapham Results

In Wilberforce and the Clapham Group, we see the rare combination of people who pursued cultural influence, a piercing prophetic message to the church and the nation, and an urgent call for people to find and follow the one true Savior of the world.

Their most recognized accomplishment was the abolition of the slave trade with the passage of the Slave Trade Act in 1807, and in 1833, the complete abolition of slavery throughout the Empire through the Slavery Abolition Act. This final piece of legislation was passed just days before Wilberforce entered his eternal home.

The Clapham Group transformed society through establishing widespread education of the poor, Sunday school improvements, measures to reduce alcoholism and gambling, regulations to improve prison conditions, improved working conditions for adults and children, the Foreign Bible Society, the Church Mission Society, and the Society for the Prevention of Cruelty to Animals.[18]

The Clapham Group chose in all things to follow Jesus' admonition to: "treat others as you would want to be treated" (Matthew 7:12). Recognizing the enormity of Wilberforce's accomplishments and that they were humanly impossible,[19] Metaxas concludes:

For the first time in history, groups sprang up for every possible social cause. Wilberforce's first "great object" was the abolition of the slave trade, but his second "great object," one might say, was the abolition of every lesser social ill ... Taken all together, it's difficult to escape the verdict that William Wilberforce was simply the greatest social reformer in the history of the world ... Frederick Douglass gushed that Wilberforce's "faith, persistence, and enthusiasm" had "thawed the British heart into sympathy for the slave, and moved the strong arm of government to, in mercy, put an end to this bondage."[20]

Because of their commitment to Christ and biblical principles, the Clapham Group witnessed the transformation of Great Britain and the British Empire.[21] The whole way of thinking about slavery, that it was economically necessary and morally defensible, collapsed throughout all of society. The very mindsets that had been embraced by every culture for millennia were replaced with another way of seeing the world. It was as if Great Britain experienced a Great Change, similar to the Great Change that Wilberforce had experienced 58 years prior.[22]

This unfolding of history sounds strangely similar to what Daniel saw in his vision: the beastly lion—perhaps the British Empire—becoming like a human being standing on two feet and receiving a reasonable mind, one which cared about humanity.

Called to Contend

Before the establishment of the Clapham Group, British Christians neglected God's call to be the salt of the earth. American Christians have done the same. We have even left expressing goodness to humanity to secular organizations and government programs by reasoning, *why get involved when they have it covered?* Why is this?

Like eighteenth-century Britain, ignorance of even the possibility of widespread societal transformation is at play. However, we have now observed substantive examples of such transformation in ancient Samaria through Philip's *life of the mind and life in Spirit ministry*; and the British Empire through Wilberforce's ambition to become the salt of the earth. Our first step is to take these accounts seriously and evaluate what they mean for us.

Second, we need to do the hard work to maintain our saltiness and seek God on how to influence those around us. Don't assume no one will listen to you. Too often, we talk ourselves out of being the salt of the earth before we have started. To be the salt of the earth, Jesus, Paul, Philip, and the Clapham Group sought God and followed His leading, even at great personal cost. We must do the same.

Third, we cannot neglect the examples of Jesus, Paul, and Philip ministering in power through the enabling of the Holy Spirit. To influence society, God's gospel and God's Word must go out in God's power, our adversary must be evicted, and at least some people must experience the healing of the living God.

Fourth, God is calling us to preserve His values in our communities. We must not outsource this call to pastors or "special" Christians, nor should we naïvely believe that God will send the next Philip or Wilberforce to save us from societal evils. Notably, an increasing number of nameless, faceless Christians are taking responsibility for cultural evil and are speaking out:

- Hundreds of Christian employees at Google circulated a petition to stop a Pride and Drag Show event due to its offensive nature. Because these Christians took Jesus' mandate seriously to be the salt of the earth, Google changed the event.[23]

- Justin, a nurse of 15 years, is standing up at his hospital, opposing the use of terms like "birthing parents," meaning either men or women can give birth. Although medical practitioners are currently debating gender fluidity, Justin's hospital is pretending consensus already exists. To protect the rights of Christians and others with traditional values working in health care, as well as promote the truth, Justin has created The Healthcare Truth and Freedom Alliance.[24]
- Bob, the senior manager of a large box store, was forced to take Critical Race Theory training. During this training, white people were disparaged by the seminar leaders because of their skin color. On the second day, Bob spoke up representing the Christian position on racism. From that point forward, the tone of the seminar became respectful of all ethnicities.

In each example, nobody waited for a national figure to save the day. Christians without a special calling or notoriety stood up for what was right in God's eyes. God's values were preserved, and the lies of the enemy—the father of lies—were rejected. In each case, Christians contended for the faith in society and made a difference.

Last, God's calling for each of us is to our own communities. What about where you live? Are you Christ's ambassador doing what He has called you to do as the salt of the earth and light of the world? After all, He is the One who called us to represent Him on every topic. Have we, can we, will we answer God's call locally?

• • •

Because the church is the radiance of Christ and exists for God's glory, our calling is not only to contend for our local churches and society. We must also influence those who govern us. It is to contend in the government sphere, the third battlefront, that we must turn our attention to next.

IN GOVERNMENT

When there is moral rot within a nation, its government topples easily. But wise and knowledgeable leaders bring stability.

Proverbs 28:2

In his book, *When a Nation Forgets God: 7 Lessons We Must Learn from Nazi Germany*, Erwin Lutzer warns that "When God is separated from government, judgment follows."[1] In other words, God will assess how far a nation's leaders have strayed from His ways and will act accordingly.

In America's case, we should find our nation's departure from the U.S. Constitution, immoral policies, laws, regulations, agencies, and the lies and immorality of those who hold public office deeply troubling. Most of our leaders, whether they know it or not, are governing in defiance of God's principles. Examples abound, but let's focus on one that is fundamental to every nation.

Parental Rights

God created marriage, encourages those in marriage to have kids, instructs parents to raise their own children, and commands children to obey their parents (Genesis 1:27–28; 2:22–24; Exodus 20:12;

Deuteronomy 6:1–9; Ephesians 5:32–6:4; Colossians 3:18–21). This is God's plan for the family. Parental rights are not something to be approved of by the government, but to be recognized apart from the government as rights that God has given to each parent. Yet, due to intrusive government, parents are facing unprecedented challenges to raise their children with the same values as they were raised. This poses a serious threat to the family—the building block of civilization.

California

Two teachers are suing their San Diego school district for prohibiting them from informing parents of their child's gender preference. Their complaint centers on school administrators instructing them to "refer to children by their preferred names and pronouns during school, but revert back to their given names and pronouns when communicating with parents."[2] One of the plaintiffs stated, "This seems crazy. This seems like the school wants to take over [being] ... the parent. And as a parent, I would not want that for my own children."[3]

Florida

Endorsed by President Biden, the nation's largest labor union, the three-million strong National Education Association (NEA), advised Florida teachers to ignore state law requiring teachers to inform parents of their child's gender preference.[4]

Washington

The State of Washington recently passed legislation to provide housing for kids whose parents do not support their choice to undergo sex reassignment surgery. Minors can now legally reject their parents' counsel and run to government housing to meet their needs.[5]

New Jersey

The New Jersey attorney general is suing three New Jersey school districts for requiring teachers and administrators to notify parents if students formally want to "change their gender identity, pronouns or name, use different bathrooms, or change the gender of teams they play on." The governor, speaking in support of the attorney general, is concerned that parents finding out that their child is non-binary may be harmful to the child.[6] The government wants to replace the parents in this life-altering decision.

Michigan

Smiling from ear to ear, Governor Gretchen Whitmer held up two freshly signed pieces of legislation, tweeting,

> As a mom of a member of the [LGBTQ] community and a proud, lifelong ally, I'm grateful that today we're banning the horrific practice of conversion therapy in Michigan. In doing so, we are taking action to make Michigan a more welcoming, inclusive place.[7]

This legislation also criminalized therapy "aimed at persuading girls they are girls and boys they are boys."[8] Again, the message to parents who believe in biblical principles, or at least traditional values, is clear: Seeking professional help for your child's gender confusion is against the law. And according to Whitmer, your belief in God's design of fixed genders is "horrific."

Parents Matter

History shows that God's design for the family is a primary target of autocrats with totalitarian ambitions. This is why Chinese Chairman Mao Zedong (1893–1976) had school children and his Red Guard high school and university students reading and enthusiastically waving *Quotations from Chairman Mao Zedong*, known worldwide as "The Little Red Book."[9] Among this group, allegiance to the government is to replace loyalty to Mom and Dad.

Xi Van Fleet migrated from China to America in 1986 and is the author of *Mao's America: A Survivor's Warning*. She explains Marxism's goal to separate children from their parents and the implications for America:

> From a very early age and in kindergarten, we were taught that our parents are just biological parents. Our real parents are the party [i.e., the government] … If there's a conflict between choosing between your own parents or the party, you should always, always choose the party… Here in [America's] school [system], especially today, you are supposed to go to trusted adults, not your parents. They did not say that in the party, but it is very similar. They want to cut the ties between the parents and the children. Why? That's how you control the children.[10]

This is why the U.S. Department of Education and other government agencies are tenaciously indoctrinating America's youth. LGBTQ lifestyles must be normalized, all white people are guilty of white privilege, and Christianity is the oppressor's religion. The elite social engineers can achieve their godless socialist utopia once the next generation eagerly supports their ideology.

In a shocking statement that caught Van Fleet's attention, President Biden stated in a speech recognizing the Teacher of the Year in 2023, "There's no such thing as someone else's child. Our nation's children are all our children."[11] As reported by *USA Today*, it is becoming increasingly common for politicians to say or imply that they, rather than parents, know what is best for kids.[12]

In response to Biden's speech, Moms for Liberty, a leading grassroots parental rights advocacy group, tweeted: "We do NOT co-parent with the government."[13]

Ideologically driven, Biden's statement was emboldened by those who previously made similar assertions. Former Virginia Governor Terry McAuliffe said in a 2021 debate: "I don't think parents should be telling schools what they should teach."[14] In 2022, the Michigan Democratic Party posted, and later deleted, on social media: "The purpose of public education in a public school is not to teach kids only what parents want them to be taught. It is to teach them what society needs them to know. The client of the public school is not the parent, but the entire community, the public."[15]

Prioritizing the collective group over the individual is classic Marxist teaching. In other words, we are told to make sacrifices for the greater good. Unfortunately, it is becoming clear that this means that the government will control the direction of humanity and will sideline parents however, whenever necessary.

Governments consistently use schools to indoctrinate the next generation toward their own political ends. Concerned about America's current environment, Rod Dreher explains:

> The family came under direct and sustained assault by the government, which saw its sovereignty as a threat to state control of all individuals ... The left-wing assault on traditional marriage and family commenced in the West with the sexual revolution in the 1960s. It continues today in the form of direct attacks by the Left, including law professors advocating legal structures that dismantle the traditional family as an oppressive institution. More ominously, it comes from policies, laws, and court decisions that diminish or sever parental rights in cases involving transgender minors.[16]

Adhering to God's design, Christians must call out government intrusion and tenaciously protect parental rights. Much is at stake.

Ignorance Abounds

Politicians campaign with big smiles, enthusiastic promises, and glowing aspirations of saving democracy and the soul of America. But, once elected, these public "servants" often lead and legislate against the very rights they promised to protect. Equally disturbing, church leadership typically does not provide congregants with the biblical framework to know what legislation is undermining God's purposes. Thus, the body of Christ sits in ignorance as the battle over who governs us and how, shifts dramatically in favor of the father of lies.

As long as there is daylight, Christians must influence elected officials to advance legislation and public policy that reflects God's will and ways. We can still influence public policy on parental rights, sex trafficking, pedophilia, gender confusion, pornography, LGBTQ indoctrination, euthanasia, abortion, national sovereignty, election integrity, the recreational use of marijuana, local and national debt, pandemic responses, censorship, and racism. The Bible provides God's answers for each of these issues and more. But if we do nothing to be the salt of the earth, the consequences will be severe.

Who Tramples Who

British author and Bible teacher Derek Prince (1915–2003) highlights Jesus' warning that salt can lose its saltiness until "it is no longer good for anything, but to be trampled by men" (Matthew 5:13). Then he asks this troubling question: But who does the trampling and why?

According to Prince, the church's failure to be the salt of the earth emboldens evil to trample a nation and, with it, the disobedient, fearful church. Either Christians will obey Jesus' directive to be salty, including in the government sphere, or we will be counted among the trampled.[17] Similarly, author and Bible teacher Timothy Zebell states:

> The heart of a forerunner is to be on the frontlines with God's timely message wherever God calls him or her and to encourage others to do the same. Certainly, this includes fighting political causes, especially when those causes are informed by a Christian worldview. In a Democratic Republic, we have a responsibility to be aware of what is happening in our government and to seek to influence it. Our heavenly charge to serve as salt and light within the world includes the realm of politics. If we entirely disengage, then we are neglecting both our Christian duty and our obligation as citizens of this country, and we will be held culpable by God for failing to uphold righteousness and for allowing evil an opportunity to succeed.[18]

Zebell goes on to explain misconceptions in the church, which led to the current LGBTQ acceptance throughout our government and culture:

> As Christians, we have a responsibility to resist evil wherever we have influence, which in our country includes the national conversation. The progression of the LGBTQ+ movement is illustrative of this. Before the Supreme Court's ruling in *Obergefell v. Hodges (2015)*, many of God's people were determined not to push back against homosexuality—and particularly the issue of homosexual marriages. These Christians determined to emphasize the positive elements of the Christian message rather than the negative, believing that the national conversation about LGBTQ+ issues would eventually subside if we would only provide the homosexual community an

opportunity to be heard. After all, the majority of Americans were, at the time, still uncomfortable with the subject of homosexuality, regardless of their religious affiliation. As such, dramatic shifts in public policy seemed unlikely. This strategy could not have proven to be more mistaken.

What Christians witnessed was an unprecedented advancement of homosexual causes in America. Activists became emboldened, intimidating politicians who increasingly felt the lack of vocal support from those who opposed homosexuality. For all practical purposes, these activists received everything they sought, and then some. However, rather than be satisfied, like so many Christians had hoped, they chose to open a new cultural battlefront: Transgender rights.[19]

Germany Again?

Erwin Lutzer explains that before Hitler rose to power, Germans had embraced the "two-sphere" approach to public policy, stating, "Christ is Lord of the church, but the Kaiser (Caesar) is, after a manner of speaking, lord over the political sphere... Indeed, allegiance to God was best demonstrated by allegiance to the State."[20]

This false dichotomy between God's domain and the government's domain largely describes the Christian worldview in America. It is as if we believe that godless leaders exercising extensive influence over culture will somehow find the truth about life and morality apart from the Bible and Christian influence. But when has the darkened mind ever been able to understand God's design and purposes for humanity? We have fooled ourselves into believing that the church's non-involvement in the public sphere will somehow turn out in humanity's favor.

Separation of Church and State

Hitler's "two sphere" approach is ominously similar to America's separation of church and state mantra. However, the phrase "separation of church and state" is not found in the U.S. Constitution nor in any of America's founding documents. Also, it is not found nor is it implied in the Bible.

This phrase originated in a short letter written by Thomas Jefferson to the Danbury Baptists Association in Connecticut. Scarcely explained in our churches, Jefferson's intent in writing this letter was not to protect the government from Christians, *but to protect Christians from the government*. Dated January 1, 1802, Jefferson wrote his letter to assure Christians that the U.S. government would not insert itself into the affairs of the church:

> Believing with you that religion is a matter which lies solely between man & his god, that he owes account to none other for his faith or his worship, that the legitimate powers of government reach actions only and not opinions, I contemplate with sovereign reverence that act of the whole American people which declared that their legislature should "make no law respecting an establishment of religion, or prohibiting the free exercise thereof;" thus building a wall of eternal separation between Church & State. Congress [is] thus inhibited from acts respecting religion, and the Executive authorised only to execute their acts, I have refrained from prescribing even those occasional performances of devotion, practiced indeed by the Executive of another nation as the legal head of its church, but subject here, as religious exercises only to the voluntary regulations and discipline of each respective sect.[21]

When politicians claim the necessity for a "thick wall between church and state" to protect the government from religious influence, they have misunderstood what Jefferson wrote or are intentionally manipulating the conversation to exclude God and religiously-based morality.

Half-Right

Lutzer explains an additional mindset held in Nazi Germany that is strangely similar to what we observe in America today:

> Within the Lutheran church there was a strong pietistic movement that advocated a return to biblical piety, the worship of God within the heart ... They witnessed to the saving grace of Christ but believed that the church's mission was only to preach Christ. Pietism, with its emphasis on personal devotion to Christ, was used to interject spiritual life into the mainstream Lutheran church. But by insisting that their faith was private and should not be brought into the political sphere, pietism had scant influence in stemming the Nazi tide.
>
> So those who dutifully tolerated the excesses of the Nazi regime, but simply continued to study the Bible to maintain a warm heart, are to be commended for getting it half-right. Certainly they were much more effective than those who ceased to study their Bibles and enthusiastically endorsed the regime. These pious Christians thought that if they left Hitler alone, he would leave them alone. But they discovered that was not possible. Hitler also put pressure on them to have their children indoctrinated in the State schools and, thanks to public pressure, their churches were not equipping members to stand against the abuses that were developing around them."[22]

We do not want to minimize the need to have warm hearts for Christ. Indeed, our love and devotion to Him are central. But once we have a strong relationship with Jesus, we must display our love and devotion for Him by contending for what is good and right.

Overcoming Negligence

Martin Luther King Jr. exhorted the church to be the conscience of the State.[23] But how is anyone's conscience pricked—in the pews or in the halls of power—when Christians say nothing? Have we believed that Christ's command to be salt and light excludes government? Are we to only contend for better worship services and personal sanctification, and not for the honesty and integrity of those who represent us?

It is as if we believe that Jesus meant to say that the kingdom of God is like a lump of leaven that permeates the entire loaf of bread (Matthew 13:33), except for the government. This misunderstanding of God's purposes has resulted in being governed by those who possess some of the most depraved minds in America.

The church cannot fulfill its God-given mission if it remains unengaged in advocating biblical morality among those who govern us. Shepherds of the flock must explain to the sheep the laws and policies that promote evil, and the laws and policies that are in alignment with God's Word. As a result of becoming informed, individuals throughout the flock will start to consider how to make a difference in government.

Not every elected official will be a Christ-follower. But for the church to fail to advocate for morally grounded candidates, candidates with common sense, and to hold those elected to office accountable for their entire term, is negligence of the worst kind.

What the Bible Says

Reading the Bible, the U.S. Constitution, and the Bill of Rights will lead us to one conclusion. There is no contradiction with Christians influencing government while the government oversees civic affairs. Paul states:

> Everyone must submit to governing authorities. For all authority comes from God, and those in positions of authority have been placed there by God. So anyone who rebels against authority is rebelling against what God has instituted, and they will be punished. For the authorities do not strike fear in people who are doing right, but in those who are doing wrong. Would you like to live without fear of the authorities? Do what is right, and they will honor you. The authorities are God's servants, sent for your good. But if you are doing wrong, of course you should be afraid, for they have the power to punish you. They are God's servants, sent for the very purpose of punishing those who do what is wrong. So you must submit to them, not only to avoid punishment, but also to keep a clear conscience. Pay your taxes, too, for these same reasons. For government workers need to be paid. They are serving God in what they do. Give to everyone what you owe them: Pay your taxes and government fees to those who collect them, and give respect and honor to those who are in authority.
>
> Romans 13:1–7

Paul warns Christians not to rebel against the government. Anyone who undermines the governing authorities or orchestrates an insurrection will find themselves fighting against the government *and God*. Yet, living in a democratic republic, advocating and persuading leaders toward truth, biblical morality, and healthy policymaking is not inciting an insurrection, nor is it rebellious. We are simply taking part in a process approved by our government, a process which honors God.

A Constitutional Republic Versus Roman Tyranny

Paul wrote the book of Romans during a time when there was no higher earthly authority than Caesar. Caesar was a law unto himself and led accordingly. But in America, all government leaders—local, state, and federal, including the President—must answer to a higher earthly authority than themselves: the U.S. Constitution.

When the Constitution is violated, U.S. citizens are well within their rights to publicly protest, vote for a better candidate, urge elected officials to pursue impeachment, or pursue other legal recourse. Our government's system of checks and balances and the protection of citizens who challenge policies and expose corruption safeguard our nation from its own leaders. Indeed, the U.S. Constitution encourages citizens to speak out and demonstrate as one's conscience leads.[24]

The Constitution also states that elected officials serve and answer to *We the People*. This was not the case when Paul wrote to the ancient Romans. America was set up for policymakers to answer to the people rather than the other way around.

God and Corruption

Paul states that the government "authorities are God's servants, sent for your good," who will punish those who do wrong. But what are we to do when the government promotes evil and rewards the wicked? The psalmist speaks to this situation:

> Can a corrupt throne be allied with you [oh God]—
> a throne that brings on misery by its decrees?

The wicked band together against the righteous
and condemn the innocent to death.

Psalm 94:20–21 NIV

Why are the righteous being put to death in this psalm? God's people are not obeying the evil decrees of the throne, that is, the seat of government, nor the dictates of a wicked culture. Notice that God Himself is not aligned with the throne. We must always follow God's commands regardless of what policies, decrees, and laws are being enforced by the government.

Biblical Examples

Two midwives, Shiphrah and Puah, were commanded by Pharaoh, the king of Egypt, to kill Hebrew boys at birth. This was Pharaoh's scheme to control the population of his slaves lest they become too numerous and overthrow him. However, Shiphrah and Puah refused to obey Pharaoh's order and allowed the Hebrew boys to live (Exodus 1:17).

Not only did Shiphrah and Puah not submit to the governing authorities, they also lied to Pharaoh about what they had done (Exodus 1:18–19). In light of this violation of the government's decree, did God punish them? Exodus records, "So God was good to the midwives, and the Israelites continued to multiply, growing more and more powerful. And because the midwives feared God, he gave them families of their own" (Exodus 1:20–21). Even when defying the government, the midwives experienced God's protection and blessing.

Daniel, Shadrach, Meshack, and Abednego demonstrated exemplary faith when they were willing to die rather than comply with the king's decrees (Daniel 3 & 6). These heroes of the faith opposed their leaders and stood for righteousness, even without the legal standing we enjoy today provided by the U.S. Constitution.

These examples underscore Prince's admonition for Christians to stand strong and be salt and light against evil, even evil in the government.

Contending Now

Contending for the faith in government is a broad topic, too broad to cover in one chapter. Yet, let us take a moment to expand on Paul's command to intercede for the government, highlight election integrity, and the importance of evaluating those running for office.

Let's Start Where Paul Did

Paul appeals to the body of Christ to "pray for kings and all those in authority" (1 Timothy 2:2). He urges us not to begin by contending with our leaders on policy matters but calls us to contend with God for our leaders.

Interceding for those who govern us is a serious undertaking for two reasons. First, Paul said that an orderly government based on truth and honesty will allow us to live peaceful and quiet lives (1 Timothy 2:2). Second, this peaceful atmosphere will help the gospel reach more people and with greater fruitfulness (1 Timothy 2:3). Are we gathering to intercede on behalf of our local, state, and federal leaders? Are we praying for our leaders by name, as well as the issues they are facing? If not, this is where we must start.

Election Integrity

A fraudulent election is not a left versus right issue. It is a good versus evil issue. The book of Proverbs explains God's position on deceptive practices: "Differing weights are an abomination to the Lord, and a false scale is not good" (Proverbs 20:10; 23). This proverb is in the cultural context of business practices, but a tabulating process that includes fraudulent ballots or one that intentionally destroys completed ballots, deletes electronic ballots, or weighs a certain candidate's ballots greater than another candidate's ballots is also a "false scale." This, too, is an abomination to God. Christians must contend for election integrity out of a sense of fairness and justice, whether or not our preferred candidate is elected.

The media and various politicians have spread the lie that voter fraud happens in every election but not to the degree that will change the results. However, with growing evil in our nation coupled with the power and policies at stake, it is hard to imagine that those who engage in such activities would try something that would not overturn elections. It is my belief that election fraud has been taking place throughout much of America's history and is successful at least some of the time.

As the salt of the earth, we must ask, what are we doing to ensure election integrity in our local communities? By contacting a county clerk, anyone can become a ballot tender, ballot challenger, or receive information on how to be part of the tabulation process.

Evaluating Candidates

It is vital that Christians inform themselves and each other to know which candidates align most closely with God's principles. The Revolutionary War was fought to ensure that the people had representation in government. We must not squander the privilege to vote—and vote for the candidate closest to a biblical worldview.

Once sworn into office, we must keep our leaders accountable. Phone calls and emails matter. Speaking at school board meetings and city council meetings matter. We must each do our part to influence policymakers.

Is It Worth It?

Lutzer explains that "when God is ousted from government," transcendent values are replaced with four destructive behaviors:
- The raw use of power
- Eroticism
- Arbitrary judicial rulings
- The morality of personal pragmaticism[25]

These indicators of God's departure are already evident throughout America. This raises important questions: Will contending for biblical morality in the government sphere have any effect? Are we already too far gone? Is contending in the government sphere a waste of time?

We often try to determine if the cost of a public stand for Christ will be worth it. Yet, it is not for us to decide whether standing up for righteousness will be worth it. Standing up publicly for anything unpopular will likely be costly with scant returns, at least in the short term. But Scripture compels us to live righteously, expose evil, and speak the truth regardless of the outcome. While we all hope to see remarkable results—and quickly—God wants us to stand with Him on every issue and leave the results to Him.

Representing God

Only a small number of Christians will aspire to and become public servants in city, county, state, or federal government. But every Christian can be God's representative to their elected officials.

A young man, Marcus Schroeder, chose to be salt and light by intending to share the gospel and a Christian perspective on sexuality at a drag queen performance at a park in Watertown, Wisconsin. State law prohibits the exposure of those twelve and younger to this kind of sexualized behavior, with modified restrictions for those thirteen to eighteen. Speaking publicly out of his love for God and kids, Schroeder was arrested.[26]

After his release, Schroeder chose to contend for God's purposes again, this time attempting to influence local officials at a Watertown City Hall meeting. His speech addressed both his own situation and the participation of a Nazi group that also attended the event. Here is Schroeder's full speech:

> I just want to ask a simple question. I know a Nazi group showed up at the event Saturday, and people were talking about that. And I just want for all of us to really think about this: What's wrong with Nazism? Like seriously, what's wrong with Nazism? Because, imagine for a moment that there is no God above us, no hell below us, no heaven to live for, as John Lennon wanted [us] to imagine. If we are truly the result of evolved stardust and our ancestors were fish and we are the descendants of monkeys, then where do we find our value as human beings? What is wrong with Nazism, unless if you understand that the God of Scripture says that we are made in His image? And so, to murder innocent people is a violation to God's commands.

As a Christian, I can say that what the Nazi's did in Nazi Germany was completely horrific and that they should have been resisted. In fact, the number one people group that resisted the Nazis were Christians. And the reason why was because they had a worldview that said that people are made in God's image and that they have worth and value. That's why Nazism is wrong. But if we are going to reject the Christian worldview, then we can't hold on to the fruit that comes from the Christian worldview, while denying the actual foundation.

Intolerance is an interesting word [as are] tolerance, hatred, love, bigotry, and things like that because every culture has something it is intolerant toward and something it is tolerant of. There are things like murder and rape and stealing and just crimes [overall] that we are intolerant toward as a society. And so every society has something it is intolerant toward. The question is: what is our object of intolerance and what is our object of tolerance?

When I showed up Saturday, all I did was read from Scripture on the sidewalk. I read from the Bible [in the book of] Galatians. By the way, I wasn't reading Romans one. I wasn't reading any passage against homosexuality or anything like that. I was reading a passage from the Bible about love and I was arrested. No reason. Not given any warning. Not told anything about my amplification needing to be turned down. I was arrested and taken into custody simply for reading the Bible on the sidewalk.

You see, as we become more and more tolerant of sexual immorality in our culture, we become more and more intolerant towards Christian morality. And the more we become intolerant toward Christian morality, the more we are going to see lawlessness in our streets. The more we become intolerant of Christian morality, the more we are going to see Nazis. The more we are going to see people who don't hold to a Christian worldview who think everybody is a result of animals, and therefore we are animals, and why can't we just act like animals?

We were called a hate group. We were told that we don't want to understand the other side. And I just want to set the record straight. I am more than happy to have that conversation with the other side. I did speech and debate throughout high school and one of the things we were taught in debate is that you can't make an argument for your side until you are able to make the argument for the other side.

I have sat down and had hours of discussion with LGBTQ activists. I completely understand the other side. I want to [further] understand the other side, but drag queens twerking on kids in lingerie is unacceptable. And that is something we have to notice as a culture. We can have our disagreements, but there comes a time when we have to understand that we are all going to stand before God one day and we are going to have to give an account for what we have done with the children in our society—the innocent minds and the children who deserve to be protected.[27]

Called to Contend

Marcus Schroeder spoke up to warn those at the park and at the City Hall meeting—Christians and non-Christians, citizens and elected officials alike. He warned his listeners of where the current evil, if left unchecked, would lead.

As Lutzer teaches, Schroeder spoke the truth humbly, yet firmly. As Jesus taught and Derek Prince exhorted, Schroeder stepped out in faith to be salt and light in his community to inspire change so as not to be trampled under the feet of evil men. As Timothy Zebell advocated,

Schroeder took responsibility for influencing culture both in the community and government spheres. Upholding the U.S. Constitution and in agreement with Paul's view of government, Schroeder appealed to his local authorities to make crucial changes in his community. We must ask, what from Schroeder's example applies to us? After all, each of us is called to be salt and light in our communities.

Contending for the radiance of Christ in our churches, contending for God's goodness and the gospel of the kingdom in society, and contending for righteousness among those who govern is God's mandate to us. Will we contend for the faith in these three spheres? Are we willing to obey God in the present, regardless of America's future? Are we willing to step out in faith to be the salt of the earth and the light of the world and leave the results to God?

• • •

If so, it is time to overcome. And it is with a vision to overcome that we conclude our journey.

TIME TO OVERCOME

Here on earth you will have many trials and sorrows. But take heart, because I [Jesus] have overcome the world.

John 16:33

I am writing this final chapter on the anniversary of 9/11, a stark reminder of our nation's dangerous trajectory. On that day more than twenty years ago, there was a breach in America's defense to warn us of our nation's waywardness and growing defiance of God. The meaning behind this shaking—to wake up the church and all of America—has long since passed into history, largely unnoticed. Americans chose to move on from a corrective judgment that could have brought us to the place of humility and deep repentance that God longs to see. Since 2001, numerous additional warnings have been ignored.

All indications show that we are no longer one nation under God but one nation in rebellion to God. Such weighty observations broke the hearts of the prophets. They should break ours as well.

Will God Be Merciful?

Despite America's defiance of God's will and ways, I am still seeking Him for a great outpouring of His Spirit. I believe that such a move of God will *not avert* what is coming but *will empower God's people through what is coming.* I remain hopeful that amid intensified shakings and judgments, as well as a gloriously revived remnant, God will take a sweeping harvest of souls.

In the end, I believe that final judgment is far more likely than a revival that will put America back on course. I urge you to join me in crying out to God for mercy. And may part of that mercy include the largest harvest of souls our nation has ever experienced. My repeated heart cry is best captured by Habakkuk:

> I have heard all about you, Lord. I am filled with awe by your amazing works. In this time of our deep need, help us again as you did in years gone by. *And in your anger, remember your mercy.*
>
> Habakkuk 3:2 (emphasis added)

God may answer our cry for mercy. He may revive His people, and there may be a widespread harvest of souls. God's very nature is to be merciful, and we should seek Him wholeheartedly for such outcomes, just as Habakkuk did. However, we must not see a momentary favorable turn of events and spiritual harvest confused with God saving America. Nations that behave the way America is behaving are not saved by God. They are destroyed by God.

What To Do

What America is facing is most unusual, even unprecedented in American history. But returning to our model forerunner, John the Baptist, we have an example of what to do.

Like John, I believe we, too, will speak of Christ's coming in glorious terms as we warn others that "even now the ax of God's judgment is poised" (Matthew 3:10; Luke 3:9). Like John, who publicly confronted Herod's sin and called upon Roman soldiers to change their wicked practices (Mark 6:18; Luke 3:14, 19), I believe that we, too, will be salt to those who govern us and be salty within our communities. I believe that we, too, will preserve God's values and make the lost thirsty for something more. Like John, who called everyone to repent (Matthew 3:1–6; Luke 3:1–20), I believe we, too, will call people to "repent and believe" the Good News (Matthew 21:32; Mark 1:1–5, 15; Luke 3:17–18). Like John, I believe we, too, will serve God in times of fruitful ministry and will also stand up to the threats of the wicked (Matthew 3:5–6; Mark 6:17–19; Luke 3:20). Like John, I believe we, too, will prepare the way of the Lord to visit our churches and communities, as well as prepare for Jesus' final "visitation" at His second coming (Luke 1:17, 76–79; Luke 3:16–18; John 1:23).

This is what forerunners do. This is what contenders do. This is what overcomers do. Do you hear God speaking to that deeper place? His deeper calling? That place of surrender to bring greater glory to God?

Greater Fruit

According to Paul, the fruit of the gospel is faith, hope, and love (1 Corinthians 13:13; Colossians 1:3–5; 1 Thessalonians 1:3). These qualities were central to sustaining Paul through his many trials and persecutions, as well as the enormous fruit that he saw. The same must be true of us.

Faith Matters

Faith inspires us to read God's Word and obey it, persevere in prayer, worship privately and corporately, live in Christian community, see miracles, and influence those around us. Our faith in God also means being full of faith. In other words, we affirm that we are following an all-powerful God who can accomplish the extraordinary through us. This is why Peter and Stephen spoke boldly to the crowds. Peter lived and continued to minister. Stephen was martyred at the hands of the wicked. Either way, we live for the glory of God.

Some quip, "The reason we have so many giants roaming the land is because we have so few giant killers." We must respond full of faith when God calls upon us to pick up our slings and five smooth stones. Good for the Stephens—those who will stand firm, full of faith, bear much fruit, and who will enter God's glory soon. Good too, for the Peters—those full of faith who will remain on earth to serve Christ a bit longer. Daily faithfulness to Christ and being full of faith are essential to overcoming.

Hope Wins

Forerunners often carry a hard message. Yet, I wake up most days with a hopeful spirit. How is this possible accounting for all that America is facing?

First, I see the value in warning people of dangers that, if not addressed, will not turn out well for them, their families, and their communities. When people respond, their decisions make an immediate difference and prepares them for the challenges ahead. When people do not respond, I am grateful to have had the opportunity to do God's work and present the truth just as the biblical prophets did.

Second, I am hopeful in the present. As long as it is daylight, people will continue to come to faith and the church can carry out its salt and light mandate in each community.

Third, by preparing now, I believe that there will be local fellowships, and even communities, that won't experience the full brunt of God's judgment. Some call these exceptional areas "places of refuge" or "places of His presence." Everyone who will humble themselves, repent, seek God wholeheartedly, and return to their first love has the possibility of living under such divine protection (Proverbs 1:20–33; Joel 2:1–17; Zephaniah 2:1–3; Revelation 18:1–4).

Far and away, shifting one's gaze from this world to the age to come creates the greatest hope. Our hope must not be in this life but in the next. When things get extremely difficult, knowing we will soon be in Christ's immediate presence will keep our struggles and battles in perspective. Even as we contend for the faith in our churches, society, and government, every battle—won or lost—should be viewed in the context of our ultimate hope in being with Christ—the certain hope that He will take us home to be with Him forever! Hope, in all of its expressions, will inspire us to overcome no matter what difficulties lie ahead.

Love Motivates

The Christian life is often motivated by glorifying Christ, the fear of the Lord, rewards, and the joy of bearing fruit. Each of these motivations are biblical and important, but our primary motivation must be to love God with all of our hearts, souls, minds, and strength (Matthew 22:36–37; Mark 12:29–30).

This command from Jesus is inspiring and attainable by walking in the Spirit. Even better, God does not intend that attaining wholehearted love for Him be a life-long self-improvement plan. When Jesus called the Christians in Ephesus to return to their first love, He exhorted them to return to their first love right away (Ephesians 2:1–7). Choosing to love God first and wholly can happen in a moment!

Think of the time when you first fell in love—perhaps it was your high school sweetheart that you have been married to for years. Did it take you decades to gradually warm up to the idea that this was a special person who captivated your heart? Did it take decades to become attracted to him or her? Did you have to force yourself to think about your new love once a day for twenty or thirty minutes in the morning before you started your busy day?

Or did you find yourself unable to stop thinking about him or her? Did you find yourself continuously hoping to run into him or her? Did you eagerly wait for the next time you were together? There is a wonderful spontaneity in love that God wants us to have with Him. Let's shift from trying to love God fully through a gradual, arduous, decades-long process to loving God fully with all our hearts today.

Wholehearted Love

When married, did you find yourself giving 50 percent of your devotion to your husband or wife? Did your devotion fluctuate between 50-95 percent, but never quite got to 100 percent? If I told my wife I am 99 percent devoted to her, she would furrow her brow and ask, "Who has the other one percent?" Too often in our relationship with God, we think it is acceptable to give portions of our hearts to Him and portions of our hearts to other loves.

In contrast, when I love my wife with all my heart, no one else has the smallest piece of my heart, and she can tell! She sees that I am "all in," and her response is wonderful. We go through life with its many joys and challenges, not frustrated with each other but synchronized to handle things together. The same must be true in our relationship with God.

One of my seminary professors taught, "The Christian life works unbelievably well at the 100 percent level, but is unbelievably frustrating and painful at any other level." This principle inspires me to love and follow God with my whole heart. Love for Him and from Him will sustain us through anything. As Paul said, "Love never gives up, never loses faith, is always hopeful, and endures through every circumstance" (1 Corinthians 13:7).

Walking in faith, hope, and love is foundational to becoming an overcomer.

William Borden

Saints like William Borden (1887–1913) inspire me to pursue extraordinary fruit and overcome no matter the cost. Born into great wealth, Borden toured Asia, the Middle East, and Europe as a high school graduation gift. God used this globetrotting to show Borden the despair of those lost without Christ and their sin-ruined lives. This experience led to Borden's decision to become a foreign missionary. Borden documented his resolve with two words in his Bible: "No Reserves." He would hold nothing back. He would live fully for Christ.

While Borden was a student at Yale College, his Christ-like example and courageous faith silenced many atheists and inspired 1,000 of the 1,300-student body to join small groups focused on prayer and Bible study. Many of these students came to faith in Christ.

Upon graduating, Borden declined several job offers and added two more words to the back of his Bible: "No Retreats." He would deny the world at every turn to follow God wholeheartedly.

After additional studies at Princeton Seminary, Borden sailed to China to pursue his missionary call. Borden first stopped in Cairo, Egypt, to learn the language of the Kansu Muslims—the group to whom he would minister in China. While in Egypt, he contracted spinal meningitis. Nearing death, Borden added two final words in the back of his Bible: "No Regrets." Within a month, Borden had died at the age of 25. He never made it to China.[1]

It is not our prerogative to decide the outcome of our lives or the fruitfulness of our ministries. It is our responsibility to live by faith and obey. Like Borden, let's live with no reserves, no retreats, and no regrets.

Time to Overcome

Jesus called five of the seven churches in Revelation to repent; however, Jesus called all seven churches to overcome. The original word for overcome conveys the ideas of living in victory, prevailing against opposition, and conquering. To Jesus, overcoming is not optional. As things in America and throughout the world escalate, we must make overcoming a top priority. How can we do this?

First, let us encourage each other that Jesus would not have called us to be overcomers if it were not possible. Second, Jesus is with us through the overcoming. He told us to "take heart" because He has already "overcome the world" (John 16:33). It should be of great encouragement that THE GREAT OVERCOMER LIVES WITHIN EACH OF US. As we make it our ambition to depend upon and follow Him wholeheartedly, there should be no doubt that you and I will also overcome. Third, if we put into practice the premise of this book, contending for the faith, by default, you and I will be overcomers. Put another way, fighting for what is good and right in God's eyes will not only make us more fruitful, it will inspire the overcoming spirit within us.

Called to Contend

Faith, hope, love, and God's call to overcome compel us to contend for the faith. And contend we will! The battle of the ages is upon us. This battle is to contend for the future of our families, churches, and our communities. This is a battle we will not avoid—nor should we want to—God Himself called us into it.

The battle of the ages is fundamentally spiritual, yet observed daily in the physical. These are not culture wars but spiritual wars of good versus evil, a battle for each person's heart and mind, a battle in which eternity for countless souls hangs in the balance.

It is a battle in which God has already weighed America and found her wanting. As it was for Nebuchadnezzar's son, Belshazzar, and all of Babylon, divine judgment is hanging in the air. And like the Babylonian Empire, the stability and future of our nation can be lost in a moment. As the Church-Society-Government Paradigm reveals, America is in a most dangerous spot.

We must remember that God has called us to seek Him first and always, stand firm, and suffer with Him and for Him. And seek Him, stand firm, and sacrifice we will! We hear William Borden's words echoing inside of us: No Reserves. No Retreats. No Regrets.

We are called to be faithful in this epic battle. We are called to warn others. We are called to be salt and light. We are called to fight for the life of the church. We are called to be a witness and conscience to our communities. We are called to choose those who govern us and hold them accountable. In brief, we are called to contend.

In the end, being called to contend has nothing to do with America or whatever nation we reside. Contending has everything to do with our faithfulness to Jesus.

And faithful we will be! We are God's people, and as forerunners to what comes next, we will contend for what is good and right. Because we are contending, we have secured our spot among those who overcome. We can do no less! We follow a great King who is out in front, and He rides a white horse into battle. We follow Him because we love Him.

And we will love Him to the end.

ABOUT THE AUTHOR

Dave Warn is the founder of *Forerunners of America*, through which he has ministered to Christians in almost every stream of the body of Christ. His extensive experience in church leadership, campus ministry, and itinerant preaching has positioned him to be a compelling voice for such a time as this.

Dave gave his life to Christ as a sophomore at St. Cloud State University. Within a few months, he found himself listening to Billy Graham preach live, challenging thousands of college students with the reality that "God has not called us to a playground, but to a battleground!" Thus, the seeds were sown in his heart to contend for the faith the rest of his life.

Dave is a graduate of Denver Seminary with an M.A. in Christian Studies, during which he studied America's Great Awakenings and God's special work of reviving His people. Over time, he realized that regardless of America's outcome, a work of God among the body of Christ, which will influence the surrounding community, is always a real possibility and worth pursuing. Indeed, it is foundational to what God has called His people to do.

Dave hosts the *Forerunners of America* podcast *INSIGHTS*, which can be found on YouTube, Rumble, Spotify, and Apple Podcasts. Created by a group of like-minded friends, he also hosts *LAST CALL: Navigating the Road to Jesus' Return*. Dave and his wife, Renae, have been married since 1992 and have two grown sons.

NOTES

Chapter 1

1. Brad Plumer, "Nine Facts About Terrorism in the United States Since 9/11," The Washington Post, September 11, 2013, accessed October 12, 2022, https://www.washingtonpost.com/news/wonk/wp/2013/09/11/nine-facts-about-terrorism-in-the-united-states-since-911.
2. Erwin Lutzer, *The Cross in the Shadow of the Crescent: An Informed Response to Islam's War with Christianity* (Eugene, OR: Harvest House, 2013) 33, 73-75, 175-178.
3. "The Future of the Global Muslim Population," Pew Research Center, January 27, 2011, accessed October 12, 2022, https://www.pewresearch.org/religion/2011/01/27/the-future-of-the-global-muslim-population.
4. "The World's Muslims: Religion, Politics, and Society," Pew Research Center, April 30, 2013, accessed October 12, 2022, https://www.pewresearch.org/religion/2013/04/30/the-worlds-muslims-religion-politics-society-overview.
5. Peniel Joseph, "Obama's Effort to Heal Racial Divisions and Uplift Black America: Barack Obama's Presidency Signaled a 'Post-Racial' America at First, But the Racial Conflict Followed Disproved That," The Washington Post, April 22, 2016, accessed October 18, 2022, https://www.washingtonpost.com/graphics/national/obama-legacy//racism-during-presidency.html.
6. The Intergovernmental Panel on Climate Change, Climate Change 2013: The Physical Science Basis, eds. Thomas Stocker, Dahe Qin, et al, (New York, NY: Cambridge University Press, 2013) v. Accessed July 16, 2022, https://www.ipcc.ch/report/ar5/wg1/.
7. Tony Owusu, "Recreational Cannabis has Reached a Tipping Point, This Is How We Got Here," MSN, February 12, 2015, accessed April 4, 2024, https://www.msn.com/en-us/money/markets/recreational-cannabis-has-reached-a-tipping-point-this-is-how-we-got-here/ar-AA1ldEsv.
8. Andrew Cohen, "The Most Important Legal Stories of 2013," The Atlantic, December 13, 2013, accessed March 22, 2022, https://www.theatlantic.com/national/archive/2013/12/the-most-important-legal-stories-of-2013/282133/.
9. ProCon.org, "History of Recreational Marijuana," Britannica, September 2, 2023, accessed April 15, 2024, https://marijuana.procon.org/history-of-recreational-marijuana.
10. "The Year in Review: The biggest stories of 2013," The Verge, December 30, 2013, accessed November 8, 2022, https://www.theverge.com/2013/12/30/5224680/the-year-in-review-the-biggest-stories-of-2013.

11. Heidi Glenn, "Losing Our Religion: The Growth Of The 'Nones'," NPR, January 14, 2013, accessed October 16, 2022, https://www.npr.org/sections/thetwo-way/2013/01/14/169164840/losing-our-religion-the-growth-of-the-nones.
12. "Religion," Gallup, accessed October 20, 2022, https://news.gallup.com/poll/1690/religion.aspx.

Chapter 2

1. Mark Creech, "What About High-profile Christians Who Renounced Their Faith," Christian Post, April 17, 2021, accessed December 3, 2022, https://www.christianpost.com/voices/what-about-high-profile-christians-who-renounced-their-faith.html.
2. Jennifer Lee. "Former Desiring God Contributor Paul Maxwell Leaves the Christian Faith," Christian Today, April 10, 2021, accessed December 3, 2022, https://www.christiantoday.com/article/former.desiring.god.contributor.paul.maxwell.leaves.the.christian.faith/136647.htm.
3. Ibid. "Rhett's Spiritual Deconstruction," Ear Biscuits, February 9, 2020, accessed December 4, 2022, https://www.youtube.com/watch?v=1qbna6t1bzw&list=PLLxmqs8vQskUw61Mo3ZAc5cSRgE_bq1hZ&index=41 ; "Link's Spiritual Deconstruction," Ear Biscuits, February 16, 2020, accessed December 4, 2022, https://www.youtube.com/watch?v=w1AZhlyoD9s&list=PLLxmqs8vQskUw61Mo3ZAc5cSRgE_bq1hZ&index=40 ; "Are WE Scared of Hell," Ear Biscuits, March 8, 2020, accessed December 4, 2022, https://www.youtube.com/watch?v=AgJjvVgdNB8&list=PLLxmqs8vQskUw61Mo3ZAc5cSRgE_bq1hZ&index=37 ; "Our Years as Missionaries," Ear Biscuits, February 2, 2020, accessed December 4, 2022, https://www.youtube.com/watch?v=2_5PG-cl9WE&t=155s.
4. C.S. Lewis, *Christian Reflections*, ed. Walter Hooper (Grand Rapids, MI: Eerdmans, 1967), 33.
5. David Satter, "100 Years of Communism—and 100 Million Dead," Wall Street Journal, November 6, 2017, accessed January 27, 2023. https://www.wsj.com/articles/100-years-of-communismand-100-million-dead-1510011810.
6. Ibid.
7. Rod Dreher, *Live Not By Lies: A Manual for Christian Dissidents* (New York City, NY: Random House, 2020), xiv.
8. Ibid.
9. Satter, "100 Years of Communism."
10. "Stalin 1879-1953," Oxford Reference. Accessed January 27, 2023. https://www.oxfordreference.com/display/10.1093/acref/9780191843730.001.0001/q-oro-ed5-00010383;jsessionid=C3110F01B209A829039259A3B5BD00F2.
11. Andrew Birch, "Europe Needs the Gospel," The Evangelical Magazine, September/October 2021, accessed January 30, 2024, https://www.evangelicalmagazine.com/article/europe-needs-the-gospel.
12. John Mulinde and Mark Daniel. *Prayer Alters: A Strategy That Is Changing*

Nations (Orlando, FL: World Trumpet Mission, 2013), 24-33.
13. "Estimated COVID-19 Burden," Centers for Disease Control and Prevention, updated August 12, 2022, accessed August 28, 2022, https://archive.cdc.gov/www_cdc_gov/coronavirus/2019-ncov/cases-updates/burden.html.
14. Joseph Mercola, "The Truth Is Coming Out About COVID Deaths," The Epoch Times., March 1, 2022, accessed March 1, 2022. Site: https://www.theepochtimes.com/the-truth-is-coming-out-about-covid-deaths_4309806.html?utm_source=Morningbrief&utm_campaign=mb-2022-03-03&utm_medium=email&est=6KyK4c4DA9MEzWlkx%2Fanj%2B102%2BOy1Rvx TntRSoZOsgXZDNTfaYAF5NvTOnwKKrVGOLRyrTxIy9axrQ%3D%3D
15. "Virus Tolls Similar Despite Governors' Contrasting Actions," The Associated Press, March 13, 2021, accessed March 14, 2021, https://www.theepochtimes.com/virus-tolls-similar-despite-governors-contrasting-actions_3732095.html?utm_source=newsnoe&utm_medium=email&email=dwarn@forerunnersofamerica.org&utm_campaign=breaking-2021-03-14-1; Marine Cathcart, "Governments Doubled Down on Lockdowns After Evidence Proved They Were Ineffective," The Epoch Times, January 24, 2023, accessed January 24, 2023, https://www.theepochtimes.com/governments-doubled-down-on-lockdowns-after-evidence-proved-they-were-ineffective-professor_5005893.html
16. Mark Tapscott, "Americans Are Suffering 'Delusional Psychosis' About CCP Virus, Psychiatrist Claims," The Epoch Times, December 2, 2020, accessed December 2, 2020, https://www.theepochtimes.com/california-psychiatrist-claims-americans-are-suffering-a-delusional-psychosis-about-ccp-virus_3601044.html?utm_source=CCPVirusNewsletter&utm_medium=email&utm_campaign=2020-12-02
17. Jeffrey A. Tucker, "To Be Ruled by Liars," The Epoch Times. January 1, 2023, accessed January 16, 2023, https://www.theepochtimes.com/mkt_app/to-be-ruled-by-liars_4988332.html?src_src=Opinion&src_cmp=opinion-2023-01-18&est=ZQUIMxjTB8VjB0CrFouHudy0Y49eKC70uih6S3ZCrWI8zyGnXTs Pcce9CHfNSGs8X%2BYKx5RTKonKdg%3D%3D
18. Charlotte Cuthbertson, "Former Harvard Prof. Martin Kulldorff: 'Science and Public Health Are Broken'," The Epoch Times, February 16, 2023, accessed February 16, 2023. https://www.theepochtimes.com/exclusive-former-harvard-prof-martin-kulldorff-science-and-public-health-are-broken_4270247.html?utm_source=Morningbrief&utm_campaign=mb-2022-02-17&utm_medium=email&est=hpT%2F23B642ENZ04acoiwDKbDcF0cVzyoGjMg%2 BhYWO1xLPHAjcstVd4Q934NxJStcisjtnaItU4L0rA%3D%3D
19. Ibid.
20. Ibid.
21. The Great Barrington Declaration, accessed January 27, 2023, https://gbdeclaration.org/view-signatures.
22. "02 SDCF 11 27 1977p Rev Richard Wurmbrand, His Testimony, Sermon," The CF Archive, July 2, 2017, accessed February 3, 2023, https://www.youtube.com/watch?v=XB_R6RnLHpE; Richard Wurmbrand, *Christ in the Communist Prisons* (New York City, NY; Coward-McCann, 1968), 218-243.

Chapter 3

1. George H.W. Bush, "State of the Union Address," Miller Center, January 29, 1991, accessed February 12, 2023, https://millercenter.org/the-presidency/presidential-speeches/january-29-1991-state-union-address.
2. George H.W. Bush, "Address to the United Nations," Miller Center, October 1, 1990, accessed February 12, 2023, https://millercenter.org/the-presidency/presidential-speeches/october-1-1990-address-united-nations.
3. Jim Hoft, "Emmanuel Macron at APEC Summit: 'We Need a Single World Order'," The Gateway Pundit, November 20, 2022, accessed February 25, 2023, https://www.thegatewaypundit.com/2022/11/emanuel-macron-apec-summit-need-single-world-order/.
4. Klaus Schwab, "Rand Paul: This Is the Danger of a One-World Government," Jessie Waters Primetime, May 26, 2022, accessed June 13, 2022, https://www.youtube.com/watch?v=KknfRwyckpM.
5. Klaus Schwab and Thierry Malleret, *COVID-19: The Great Reset* (Centerport, NY: Forum Publishing, 2020) 22-26, 159-171.
6. Ibid,185-190.
7. "Environmental, Social, and Governance" Wikipedia, accessed February 26, 2023, https://en.wikipedia.org/wiki/Environmental,_social,_and_corporate_governance
8. The Forum of Young Global Leaders, https://www.younggloballeaders.org/community. Accessed March 2, 2023; "World Economic Forum's 'Young Global Leaders' Revealed," Covert Geopolitics, February 22, 2022, accessed March 3, 2023. https://geopolitics.co/2022/02/22/world-economic-forums-young-global-leaders-revealed/.
9. "The Paris Agreement," United Nations, accessed March 3, 2023, https://www.un.org/en/climatechange/paris-agreement.
10. "The League of Nations," Wikipedia, accessed March 3, 2023, https://en.wikipedia.org/wiki/League_of_Nations.
11. "United Nations Charter," United Nations, accessed March 3, 2023, https://www.un.org/en/about-us/un-charter/full-text.
12. Matthew Bell, "Why is the Strasbourg Parliament Based on Tower of Babel," Matthew Bell, June 19, 2016, accessed April 22, 2024, https://mattbell.org/why-is-the-strasbourg-parliament-based-on-tower-of-babel#%3A~%3Atext%3D%27EU%20uses%20biblical%20symbols%27%26text%3DThis%20building%20is%20based%20on%2Cuncanny%20resemblance%20to%20Bruegel%27s%20masterpiece.
13. Ibid.
14. George Washington, "From George Washington to Brigadier General Thomas Nelson, Jr.," National Archives, August 20, 1778, accessed March 15, 2023, https://founders.archives.gov/documents/Washington/03-16-02-0373.
15. Stephanie Hertzenberg, "7 Moments of Divine Intervention in U.S. History," Beliefnet. July 27, 2022, accessed Marh 16, 2023, https://www.beliefnet.com/news/7-moments-of-divine-intervention-in-us-history.aspx.
16. Ibid. Also see "13 Facts About the Battle of Long Island," Have Fun

with History, May 16, 2023, accessed October 16, 2023, https://www. havefunwithhistory.com/facts-about-the-battle-of-long-island/.
17. Brian Mashburn, "God's Providence in American History." RenewaNation, October 31, 2018, accessed March 16, 2023, https://www.renewanation.org/post/god-s-providence-in-american-history.
18. Hertzenberg, "7 Moments of Divine Intervention in U.S. History."
19. Ibid.
20. Ibid.
21. Ibid.

Chapter 4

1. John MacArthur, "When God Abandons a Nation," Grace to You, August 20, 2006, accessed July 17, 2023, https://www.gty.org/library/sermons-library/80-314/when-god-abandons-a-nation.
2. Richard Ritenbaugh, "What the Bible Says About Cyrus," Bible Tools, accessed February 14, 2023, https://www.bibletools.org/index.cfm/fuseaction/topical.show/RTD/cgg/ID/323/Cyrus.htm; John Walvoord, "The Rise and Fall of Babylon," The Nations in Prophecy, accessed February 16, 2023, https://bible.org/seriespage/5-rise-and-fall-babylon; "King Cyrus of Persia," Bible History, accessed February 16, 2023, https://www.biblehistory.net/newsletter/cyrus.htm.
3. Erwin Lutzer, *Is God on America's Side?* (Chicago, IL: Moody Publishers, 2008) 17-20.
4. Leonard Ravenhill, *Sodom had No Bible* (Pensacola, FL: Christian Life Books, 1971) 31-32.

Chapter 5

1. Passages that reveal that God uses the Church-Society-Government Paradigm to assess the status of a nation include: 1 Samuel 12:1-24; 1 Kings 8:1-11; 19:15-21; 2 Kings 11:17-20; 23:1-3; 1 Chronicles 11:1-3; 2 Chronicles 5:1-7:22; 29:1-31:30; 34:29-35:19; Ezra 1:1-10:17; Nehemiah 2:16; 5:13; 9:34-35; 11:1-36; Isaiah 9:13-17; Jeremiah 1:17-19; 2:5-8, 26; 8:1-2; 13:13; 29:1-7, 15-32; 34:1-22; 52:12-13, 24-25; Ezekiel 7:26-27; 21:1-17; 22:1-31; 29:1-16; 30:13-19; Lamentations 2:5-14, 19-22; Hosea 5:1; Haggai 1:1-15; 2:1-4; Zephaniah 1:4-18; 3:1-11; Luke 23:13; Acts 3:11-4:31.
2. Ben Carpenter, "Leaving the Problem to Others," Foundation for Economic Education, October 1, 1968, accessed October 28, 2023, https://fee.org/articles/leaving-the-problem-to-others/.
3. Stephen Turley, "Immigration and the Church: A Christian Response to the Current Border Crisis," The Imaginative Conservative, July 25, 2014, accessed March 8, 2023. https://theimaginativeconservative.org/2014/07/illegal-immigrants-church-christian-response-current-border-crisis.html.
4. Julia Ainsley, "Migrant Border Crossings in Fiscal Year 2022 Topped 2.76 Million, Breaking Previous Record," NBC News, October 22, 2022, accessed March 8, 2023. https://www.nbcnews.com/politics/immigration/migrant-border-crossings-fiscal-year-2022-topped-276-million-breaking-rcna53517.
5. The House Committee on Homeland Security Report, "Final FY23 Numbers

Show Worst Year at America's Borders—Ever," October 26, 2023, accessed February 16, 2024, https://homeland.house.gov/2023/10/26/factsheet-final-fy23-numbers-show-worst-year-at-americas-borders-ever/.
6. Lydia Saad, "Four in 10 Americans Still Highly Concerned About Illegal Immigration," April 19, 2022, Accessed March 8, 2023. https://news.gallup.com/poll/391820/four-americans-highly-concerned-illegal-immigration.aspx.
7. Alliance Defending Freedom, "Mapping Abortion Laws by State," Alliance Defending Freedom, August 25, 2022, revised January 24, 2024, accessed April 11, 2024, https://adflegal.org/article/mapping-abortion-laws-state?sourcecode=10024836_r800.
8. Ibid.
9. Gen. 9:4-6; Deut. 19:13, 21:9; 2 Kings 21:16, 24:3-4; Psa. 106:37-39; Pro. 6:17; Isa. 5:7, 26:21, 59:3-7; Jer. 2:34, 19:4-6, 22:3, 17, 26:15; Lam. 4:13; Eze. 7:23, 9:9, 16:38, 22:1-13, 27, 23:36-39; 24:6-14, 33:25-26, 35:3-9; Joel 3:19.
10. Joe Biden, "Biden Signs Respect for Marriage Act Protecting Same-sex and Interracial Marriages," PBS News Hour, December 13, 2022, accessed January 3, 2023, https://www.youtube.com/watch?v=wJ6GJCddL90.
11. Ibid.
12. Jay Clemons, "Gallup Poll - Rate of US Adults Identifying as LGBTQ Doubles in a Decade" Newsmax, February 22, 2023, accessed April 7, 2023, https://www.newsmax.com/newsfront/gallup-survey-lgbtq/2023/02/22/id/1109739/.
13. Ibid.
14. George Barna, "American Worldview Inventory 2023 - Release #1: Incidence of Biblical Worldview Shows Significant Change Since the Start of the Pandemic," Cultural Research Center at Arizona Christian University, February 28, 2023, accessed April 7, 2023, https://www.arizonachristian.edu/culturalresearchcenter/research/.
15. Ibid.

Chapter 6

1. https://teenchallengeusa.org
2. https://www.globaltc.org/our-history/
3. https://teenchallengeusa.org/news/nationwide-study-confirms-adult-teen-challenge-program-success
4. David Wilkerson, *America's Last Call*. (Lindale, TX: Wilkerson Trust Publications, 1998), 11.
5. Jeremiah 7:16; 11:14; 14:11–12, 15:1.
6. Wilkerson, *America's Last Call*, 19.
7. Also see Hosea 8:14 and Deuteronomy 8:11-14.
8. Hosea 4:2, 5:5, 10:13–15; 11:12; 13:16.
9. Hosea 1:6, 9; 2:4; 5:14; 8:13–14; 9:15; 10:7–10; 13:16.
10. Jonathan Cahn, *The Return of the Gods* (Lake Mary, FL: Frontline, 2022) 33.
11. Ibid, 24.
12. Ibid, 26.
13. Ibid, 6-7.
14. Ibid, 39-41.

15. Stone v. Graham, 449 U.S. 39 (1980). https://supreme.justia.com/cases/federal/us/449/39/.
16. Cahn, *Return of the Gods*, 43-44; Also see The Bible & Public Schools: A First Amendment Guide. Published by The National Bible Association and First Amendment Center. 1999. https://www2.kenyon.edu/Depts/Religion/Fac/Adler/Politics/Bible-in-Schools.htm#:~:text=The%20U.S.%20Department%20of%20Education%20guidelines%20reiterate%20that%20public%20schools,of%20religion%20in%20a%20public.
17. Cahn, *The Return of the Gods*, 46.
18. Ibid, 35, 39, 73-75, 95-96.
19. Ibid, p. 41.
20. Ibid, 73-74.
21. Ibid, 78.
22. Ibid 79.
23. Ibid, 117-129.
24. Ibid, 95-97.
25. Ibid, 112.
26. Jack Hobbs, "Sam Smiths Satanic Grammy's Performance Slammed on Twitter," The New York Post, February 6, 2023, accessed February 12, 2023, https://nypost.com/2023/02/06/sam-smiths-satanic-grammys-performance-slammed-on-twitter/.
27. For a less offensive description and summary of Sam Smith and Kim Petras' performance of Unholy at the 2023 Grammy Awards, go to https://www.youtube.com/watch?v=VlXIdtIBr8E. Posted February 7, 2023. Also, see Sam Smith and Kim Petras earlier Unholy performance posted September 29, 2022 with 232 million views at https://www.youtube.com/watch?v=Uq9gPaIzbe8.
28. Judah Marx and Dave Warn, "Battling Paganism," INSIGHTS, January 27, 2023, accessed January 27, 2023, https://www.youtube.com/watch?v=02Q5BMtQPS0&t=2s.
29. Deuteronomy 18:9–14; 32:17; 2 Kings 17:15–16; Psalm 106:36–37.
30. Timothy Zebell, "Stop Pining for the Good Old Days," Forerunners of America, March 21, 2023, accessed March 25, 2023, https://forerunnersofamerica.com/article/stop-pining-for-the-good-old-days.
31. Hannah Grossman, "Pentagon Doctors Claim 7-Year-Olds Can Make Decisions to Be Injected with Hormones, Puberty Suppressants," Fox News, March 22, 2023, accessed March 29, 2023, https://www.foxnews.com/media/pentagon-doctors-claim-7-year-olds-can-make-decisions-injected-hormones-puberty-suppressants.
32. Eric Metaxas, *Letter to the American Church* (Washington DC: Salem Books, 2022) xi-xii.
33. Rod Dreher, *Live Not By Lies: A Manuel for Christian Dissidents* (New York City, NY: Sentinel, 2020) 152-155, 193.
34. Ibid, 172-173.
35. David Wilkerson, *Put the Trumpet to Thy Mouth* (Springdale, PA: Whitaker House, 1985), 46.

Chapter 7

1. Robert Wilken, *The Spirit of Early Christian Thought: Seeking the Face of God* (New Haven: Yale University Press, 2005), introduction.
2. Ibid.
3. Acts 2:42; 3:1; 10:9, 30-31. As Christianity spread, some Christians added other set times of daily prayer. Paul Bradshaw, Daily Prayer in the Early Church: A Study of the Origin and Early Development of the Divine Office (Eugene, OR: Wipf & Stock, 2008), 2. Henry Chadwick, The Early Church, (Grand Rapids, MI: Eerdmans, 1968), 272-73.
4. See Luke 18:1-8, 1 Timothy 5:5-6. When Jesus taught his disciples to cry out to God "day and night," this pattern of morning and evening prayer was probably what he had in mind given the prayer practices of His day and the Old Testament background (Exodus 29:38-41; Joshua 1:8; Psalm 1:2; 1 Thessalonians 3:9-10; 2 Timothy 1:3). Also, among other requirements, Timothy was instructed only to help widows who showed up for morning and evening prayer gatherings, (1 Timothy 5:5-6).
5. For example, leaders of the First Great Awakening were known to maintain these patterns. William Wilberforce and his friends had a pattern of seeking God three hours a day, 5 a.m., noon, and 5 p.m.. D. Bruce Handmarsh, The Spirit of Early Evangelicalism: True Religion in a Modern World (New York: Oxford University Press, 2018). G. R. Balleine, A History of the Evangelical Party in the Church of England (New York: Longmans, Green, and Co., 1908), 148-9.
6. This timing of morning and evening times seeking God is estimated based on the fact that these times are referred to as "the hour of prayer" (e.g., Acts 3:1) and by the substance of their prayer times, which included certain recited passages and prayers as well as spontaneous prayers and worship. Their culture was more event-based than time-based, so the length of their meetings was probably not pre-determined and consistent.
7. For more on this subject, including other specific ways to seek God, understanding of legalism, and what is needed to advance God's kingdom, see ChristianUnion.org/7keys. https://www.christianunion.org/get-involved/seeking-god/seven-keys-to-kingdom-advancement.
8. https://www.christianunion.org/get-involved/seeking-god/three-spiritualities#Seven_Principles. Also, see Seeking God Lifestyle by Christian Union.

Chapter 8

1. John Eldredge, *Free to Live: The Utter Relief of Holiness* (New York City, NY: FaithWords, 2014) 104-110, 122-125, 159-168.
2. The Hebrew and Greek words for epidemic and pandemic are often translated into our modern English Bibles as pestilence or plague.
3. A.W. Tozer, "Spiritual Appraisers," The Alliance, March 24, 2009, accessed May 12, 2023, https://www.cmalliance.org/devotions/tozer?id=966
4. Luke 20:35-36; John 1:12; I Corinthians 6:18; Galatians 4:4-7; Ephesians 1:3-6; 2 Corinthians 5:17; Colossians 2:13-14; 1 Corinthians 2:16.

5. John 5:24; Romans 5:10; 2 Corinthians 5:18-19; Colossians 1:21-23; 2 Corinthians 5:18-20; Romans 8:35-39.
6. Paul Horrocks, "Biblical Courage," INSIGHTS, February 13, 2022, accessed May 18, 2023, https://www.youtube.com/watch?v=Yw0Ax9s1gCI&t=607s
7. Ibid.
8. Paul Horrocks and David Horrocks, *Tough Guys of the Bible: Learn the Traits of Courageous Men Who Truly Follow God* (Collierville, TN; Innovo Publishing, 2021) 53-55.
9. Ibid.

Chapter 9

1. John Grooters, "Preparing for Persecution," INSIGHTS, September 22, 2023, accessed September 25, 2023, https://www.youtube.com/watch?v=eafX6v8qx-o.
2. Billy Hallowell, "Ex-Muslim Couple in Uganda Reportedly Murdered After Converting to Christianity," Faithwire, February 19, 2024, accessed February 19, 2024, https://www.faithwire.com/2024/02/19/pray-ex-muslim-couple-in-uganda-reportedly-murdered-after-converting-to-christianity/?inid=883eebc0-7f5b-eb11-b823-005056af0da1.
3. "Trends," Open Doors, accessed May 2, 2023, https://www.opendoorsus.org/en-US/persecution/persecution-trends.
4. Corrie Ten Boom, "Corrie Ten Boom's Letter to the Western Church - 1974," Narrow Path Joys, November 1, 2014, accessed April 30, 2023, https://narrowpathjoys.org/2014/11/01/corrie-ten-booms-letter-to-the-western-church/.
5. The Associated Press, "FDA Approves Computer Chip for Humans," NBC News, October 13, 2004, accessed December 21, 2023, https://www.nbcnews.com/health/health-news/fda-approves-computer-chip-humans-flna1C9445874.
6. Ahmed Banafa, "Microchips in Humans: Consumer-Friendly App, or New Frontier in Surveillance," The Bulleting of Atomic Sciences, September 8, 2022, accessed December 21, 2023, https://thebulletin.org/premium/2022-09/microchips-in-humans-consumer-friendly-app-or-new-frontier-in-surveillance.
7. Bryan Jung, "G20 Announces Plan to Impose Digital Currencies and IDs Worldwide," September 22, 2023, accessed November 15, 2023, https://www.globalresearch.ca/g20-announces-plan-impose-digital-currencies-ids-worldwide/5832785.
8. CBS News New York, "China Assigns Every Citizen A 'Social Credit Score' To Identify Who Is And Isn't Trustworthy," CBS News, April 24, 2018, accessed April 26. 2023. https://www.cbsnews.com/newyork/news/china-assigns-every-citizen-a-social-credit-score-to-identify-who-is-and-isnt-trustworthy/.
9. "Worldwide Social Credit Industry - Infrastructure to Support Social Credit Systems Represents a $16.1 Billion Opportunity by 2026," Business Wire. December 23, 2021, accessed December 21, 2023, https://www.businesswire.com/news/home/20211223005270/en/.
10. Ibid.
11. Joseph Mercola, "Is This Why Chase Debanked Dr. Mercola?" Dr. Mercola's Censored Library, December 5, 2023, accessed December 6, 2023, https://

takecontrol.substack.com/p/is-this-why-chase-debanked-dr-mercola.
12. Ibid.
13. Ibid.
14. Daniel Payne, "Canada Shows Us that It's Time to Prepare for the Worst," Not the Bee, February 15, 2022, accessed January 17, 2024, https://notthebee.com/article/canada-shows-us-that-its-time-to-prepare-for-the-worst.
15. Jordan Peterson and Scott Jensen, "Tyranny through Weaponized Bureaucracy with Scott Jensen," Jordan B. Peterson, April 17, 2023, accessed April 23, 2023, https://www.youtube.com/watch?v=0YRMajzRKU8.
16. Liz Collin, "Nurse Turned Whistleblower Speaks Out on Health Care Corruption," Alpha News, April 18, 2023, accessed May 4, 2023, https://www.youtube.com/watch?v=Iuw-Ap8OQHE; Chester Tam, "Former ICU Nurse Shares Insights on COVID Protocols and Vaccine-Related Concerns," Chester Tam Substack, December 15, 2023, accessed April 17, 2024, https://chestermtam.substack.com/p/former-icu-nurse-shares-insights.
17. Ibid.
18. Ibid.
19. Lutzer Erwin, *The Church in Babylon* (Chicago, IL: Moody, 2018), 151.
20. Spencer Lindquist, "Trans Activists Pushed Aggressive Rhetoric Before Shooting at Christian School," Breitbart, March 28, 2023, accessed April 27, 2023, https://www.breitbart.com/crime/2023/03/28/trans-activists-pushed-aggressive-rhetoric-before-shooting-at-christian-school/
21. Ibid.
22. Joseph Biden, "A Proclamation on Transgender Day of Visibility," The White House, March 30, 2023, accessed April 3, 2023, https://www.whitehouse.gov/briefing-room/presidential-actions/2023/03/30/a-proclamation-on-transgender-day-of-visibility/.
23. Ibid.

Chapter 10

1. Art Katz, "And They Crucified Him," Ellerslie Discipleship Training, August 29, 2009, accessed May 17, 2023, https://www.youtube.com/watch?v=2XK1xpKRWyQ.
2. For Paul's case against this heresy and what to do, see Romans 6:1–23.
3. Williams Institute, "More than 40% of Transgender Adults in the US have Attempted Suicide," July 20, 2023, accessed December 26, 2023. https://williamsinstitute.law.ucla.edu/press/transpop-suicide-press-release. This study concludes that the reason for higher risk factors for transgender people is because of: "A lack of societal recognition and acceptance of gender identities outside of the binary of cisgender man or woman and increasing politically motivated attacks on transgender individuals, increase stigma and prejudice and related exposure to minority stress, which contributes to the high rates of substance use and suicidality we see among transgender people." However, based on the Bible, I believe the reason that there are higher rates of suicide and substance abuse within the transgender community is because trans people are trying to change how God created them.

4. William Sey. "You're Fearfully and Wonderfully De-trans." Posted July 5. 2023. https://www.christianpost.com/voices/youre-fearfully-and-wonderfully-de-trans.html.

Chapter 11

1. Aaron Earls, "Protestant Church Closures Outpace Openings in U.S.," May 25, 2021, accessed July 20, 2023, https://research.lifeway.com/2021/05/25/protestant-church-closures-outpace-openings-in-u-s/
2. Much of God's Word contrasts those who follow God wholeheartedly and anticipate rewards versus those who disobey His warnings and will face the consequences. In the context of God's commands, precepts, and judgments the psalmist says, "They are a *warning* to your servant, a *great reward* for those who obey them." (Psa. 19:11, italics mine).
3. Richard Gehman, "The East African Revival," 1986. Accessed January 10, 2024, https://repository.globethics.net/handle/20.500.12424/235855.
4. Ibid.
5. Ibid.
6. Ibid.
7. Ibid.
8. Norman Grubb, *Continuous Revival: The Secret of Victorious Living* (Fort Washington: CLC Publications, 1952) 20-24, 35-50.
9. Gehman, "The East African Revival."
10. Voddie Baucham Jr., *Fault Lines: The Social Justice Movement and Evangelicalism's Looming Catastrophe* (Washington DC: Salem Books, 2021) 207.
11. Ibid., p. 218.
12. Ibid., p. 219.
13. Patrisse Cullors and Melina Abdullah, "A Prayer for the Runner by Patrisse Cullors" Fowler Museum at UCLA, June 15, 2020, accessed June 28, 2020, https://www.youtube.com/watch?v=udEnerFMVaY.
14. Ibid.
15. "How Will Christians Respond to the Next Pandemic," INSIGHTS, October 28, 2022, accessed October 28, 2022, https://www.youtube.com/watch?v=T8k7xZchaoM.

Chapter 12

1. Louis Evan, *The Kingdom Is Yours* (Westwood, NJ: Fleming H. Revell Company: 1952) 14-15.
2. "List of Largest Empires," accessed August 8, 2023, https://en.wikipedia.org/wiki/List_of_largest_empires.
3. Eric Metaxas, *Amazing Grace: William Wilberforce and the Heroic Campaign to End Slavery* (San Fransisco, CA: HarperSanFrancisco, 2007) 69-72.
4. Ibid., 72-76.
5. Ibid., 49.
6. G. R. Balleine, *A History of the Evangelical Party in the Church of England* (New York: Longmans, Green, and Company, 1908), 148-149.
7. Metaxas, *Amazing Grace*, p. 83.

8. Metaxas, *Amazing Grace*, xvi.
9. Ibid, 85.
10. Ibid, 85.
11. Ibid, 78.
12. Ibid, 65.
13. Ibid, 79.
14. Ibid, 81-86.
15. Ibid, 169.
16. Ibid, 168-172.
17. Ibid, 170-171.
18. Ibid, 251-253.
19. Ibid, 85.
20. Ibid, xvi-xviii.
21. Ibid, 186.
22. Ibid, xv, 233.
23. Katerine Donlevy, "Google Drops Drag Show Sponsorship in Wake of Christian Employee Petition," July 27, 2023, accessed August 12, 2023, https://nypost.com/2023/06/27/google-drops-drag-show-sponsorship-after-christian-employee-petition/.
24. "Is Transgenderism Taking Root in Our Hospitals?" Forerunners of America, July 28, 2023, accessed July 28, 2023, https://www.youtube.com/watch?v=aurntCsO4Uw&t=1s.

Chapter 13

1. Erwin Lutzer, *When a Nation Forgets God: 7 Lessons We Must Learn from Nazi Germany* (Chicago, IL: Moody, 2010) 15.
2. Tré Goins-Phillip, "Teacher Claims She Was Told to Mislead 'Suspicious' Parents About Kids' Gender Identities, Now She's Suing the School," Faithwire, May 4, 2023, accessed August 4, 2023, https://www.faithwire.com/2023/05/04/teacher-claims-she-was-told-to-mislead-suspicious-parents-about-kids-gender-identities-now-shes-suing-the-school/?inid=883eebc0-7f5b-eb11-b823-00-5056af0da1.
3. Hannah Grossman, "Christian Teachers Still Locked Out of the Classroom After Refusing to 'Lie to Parents'," Fox News, December 11, 2023, accessed December 11, 2023, https://www.foxnews.com/media/christian-teachers-still-locked-out-classroom-after-refusing-lie-parents-lawsuit.
4. Libby Emmons, "Biden-backed Teacher Union Launches National LGBTQ Indoctrination Initiative," The Post Millennial, July 11, 2023, accessed August 4, 2923, https://thepostmillennial.com/exclusive-biden-backed-teacher-union-launches-national-lgbtq-indoctrination-initiative.
5. Patty McMurray, "Washington State Passes Bill Allowing Government to Take Away Minor From Parents If They Refuse To Agree to Gender Transition Surgery," Gateway Pundit, April 14, 2023, accessed July 31, 2023, https://www.thegatewaypundit.com/2023/04/washington-state-passes-bill-allowing-government-to-take-away-minor-from-parents-if-they-refuse-to-agree-to-gender-transition-surgery/.

6. Priscilla DeGregory and Katherine Donlevy, "NJ School Districts Temporarily Blocked from Enforcing Requirement to Notify Parents If Child Changes Gender Identity," New York Post, August 18, 2023, accessed April 9, 2024, https://nypost.com/2023/08/18/nj-school-districts-suffer-legal-setback-in-fight-for-parental-rights-against-state.
7. Jack Montgomery, "Michigan Gov's 'Conversion Therapy' Ban Criminalizes Parents Who Don't Affirm Transgenderism," The National Pulse, July 27, 2023, accessed July 28, 2023, https://thenationalpulse.com/2023/07/27/michigan-govs-conversion-therapy-ban-criminalizes-parents-who-dont-affirm-transgenderism.
8. Ibid.
9. Janis Mackey Fayer, "China Is Not Celebrating Cultural Revolution's 50th Anniversary," NBC News, May 13, 2016. Accessed August 4, 2023, https://www.nbcnews.com/news/china/china-not-celebrating-cultural-revolution-s-50th-anniversary-n571951.
10. Jan Jekielek, "The Dark Parallels of China's Cultural Revolution and Today's America: Survivor Xi Van Fleet," American Thought Leaders, Interview, October 28, 2023, accessed November 15, 2023, https://www.theepochtimes.com/epochtv/the-dark-parallels-of-chinas-cultural-revolution-and-todays-america-survivor-xi-van-fleet-5517619?src_src=News&src_cmp=breaking-2023-10-29-2&est=o785VwHEvce8ld%2FJqdUBjEvQNuwkHTJP%2FyaZ7nF8YCXhMUqVGPGTtHEdGFh2KBvKiWXDO3UAVpzK8Q%3D%3D.
11. Ibid.
12. Ingrid Jacques, "Who Knows What's Best for Kids? Hint: Biden and Democrats Don't Think It's Parents," USA Today, April 27, 2023, accessed January 24, 2024, https://www.usatoday.com/story/opinion/columnist/2023/04/27/biden-government-dictate-kids-education-schools-not-parents/11743676002.
13. Twitter. Moms for Liberty. April 24, 2023. Accessed January 24, 2024, https://twitter.com/Moms4Liberty/status/1650597054886846491?s=20.
14. Corey DeAngelis, Twitter, October 26, 2021, accessed January 24, 2024. https://twitter.com/DeAngelisCorey/status/1453179215101181952.
15. Jacques, "Who Knows What's Best for Kids?"
16. Dreher, *Live Not By Lies*, 132.
17. Derek Prince, "Goodness! Salt, Light and a City on a Hill - Living as Salt and Light Part 1A," Derek Prince Ministries, July 7, 2023, accessed December 8, 2023, https://www.youtube.com/watch?v=gQR_xgNcoCk; Also see www.DerekPrince.com.
18. Zebell, *The Heart of a Forerunner*, 98.
19. Ibid, 98-99.
20. Lutzer, *When a Nation Forgets God*, 17.
21. Thomas Jefferson, "Jefferson's Letter to the Danbury Baptists," Library of Congress, June 1998, accessed August 20, 2023, https://www.loc.gov/loc/lcib/9806/danpost.html.
22. Lutzer, *When a Nation Forgets God*, 17-18.
23. Martin Luther King Jr., "A Knock at Midnight," The Martin Luther King Jr. Research and Education Institute, July 1, 1962, accessed May 27, 2024, https://kinginstitute.stanford.edu/king-papers/documents/draft-chapter-vi-knock-

midnight#:~:text=The%20church%20must%20be%20reminded,bread%20for%20men%20at%20midnight.
24. The Rutherford Institute, *The Right to Protest* (Charlottesville, VA: Rutherford Institute, 2017) 1, 11. A free PDF can be downloaded at: https://www.rutherford.org/publications_resources/legal_features/constitutional_qa_the_right_to_protest.
25. Lutzer, *When a Nation Forgets God*, 27.
26. Joel Abbott, "Wisconsin Police Arrest Young Christians Protesting Drag Queen Event for Kids," Not the Bee, August 2, 2023, accessed August 3, 2023, https://notthebee.com/article/wisconsin-police-arrest-young-christians-protesting-drag-queen-event-for-kids; Steve Warren, "Arrested - Simply for Reading the Bible: Police Detain 4 Young Christians at Drag Queen Event," CBN, August 3, 2023, accessed August 3, 2023, https://www2.cbn.com/news/us/arrested-simply-reading-bible-police-detain-4-young-christians-drag-queen-event
27. Ben Zeisloft, "Marcus Schroeder City Council Speech," Twitter, August 2, 2023, accessed August 3, 2023, https://twitter.com/BenZeisloft/status/1686832065747030017?ref_src=twsrc%5Etfw%7Ctwcamp%5Etweetembed%7Ctwterm%5E1686832065747030017%7Ctwgr%5Eaaffce56ebd388fc3819d29f4b3f1c68a8152520%7Ctwcon%5Es1_c10&ref_url=https%3A%2F%2Fnotthebee.com%2Farticle%2Fwatch-young-man-arrested-for-protesting-drag-event-aimed-at-kids-shares-the-gospel-with-city-council.

Chapter 14

1. Howard Culbertson, "William Borden – No Reserves, No Retreats, No Regrets," Southern Nazarene University, accessed September 11, 2023, https://home.snu.edu/~hculbert/regret.htm; Also see Mrs. Howard Taylor, *Borden of Yale: The Wealthy American Whose Sacrifice Touched Egypt and the World for Christ* (Minneapolis, MN: Bethany House, 1988).

OTHER BOOKS BY DAVE WARN

Books Available on Amazon

America in the Balance:
God's Perspective on Nations and What to Do
By Dave Warn with Timothy Zebell

Bring the biblical principles of *Called to Contend* into your small group through the *America in the Balance* teacher's guide, or personally deeper through the individual guide!

By Dave Warn with Timothy Zebell, *America in the Balance: God's Perspective on Nations and What to Do* is a user-friendly Bible study to bring the biblical teaching of nations alive. Especially through the teacher's guide, America in the Balance provides an interactive, practical approach to learning for those in small groups and Sunday school classes.

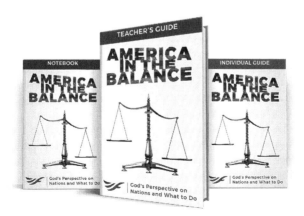

Insurgence:
The Revolutionary Nature of the Kingdom of God
By Dave Warn and Timothy Zebell

Even when things appear chaotic, God is present, stable, and has a plan. This study will answer:
- What is the kingdom of God?
- Is the kingdom of God a reality on earth today?
- Why is the kingdom of God revolutionary?
- What aspects of kingdom authority has God given to us already?

Insurgence is designed for small groups and adult Sunday school classes, as well as for individual study. In group settings, this course is ideal for those who want to lay a theologically sound foundation to minister with dramatically more fruitfulness, using biblically based, discussion-oriented material.

Heart of a Forerunner:
How to Become a Relevant and Influential Voice in a Wayward Nation
By Timothy Zebell, Foreword by Dave Warn

It is foolish to imagine that we can be disciples of a Revolutionary without being revolutionary ourselves. As Christians, we are not called to simply keep our heads low, refusing to draw attention or distinguish ourselves from a culture that is hostile to our faith. Instead, we are to imitate Jesus, whose teaching and lifestyle was so countercultural that it captured everyone's attention, from the lowliest beggar to the most powerful leaders.

- Discover God's redemptive role for nations.
- Honestly evaluate our nation's perilous trajectory.
- Learn how to verbalize your concerns.
- Learn how to become a cultural influencer.
- Learn how to prepare for difficulty.
- Learn how to minister in all circumstances.

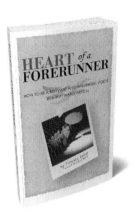

Made in the USA
Middletown, DE
01 December 2024

65843297R00150